Name: _____

CEM

Mathematics

11+
Practice
Papers

David E Hanson

GALORE
PARK

AN HACHETTE UK COMPANY

Every effort has been made to trace all copyright holders, but if any have been inadvertently overlooked, the Publishers will be pleased to make the necessary arrangements at the first opportunity.

Although every effort has been made to ensure that website addresses are correct at time of going to press, Galore Park cannot be held responsible for the content of any website mentioned in this book. It is sometimes possible to find a relocated web page by typing in the address of the home page for a website in the URL window of your browser.

Hachette UK's policy is to use papers that are natural, renewable and recyclable products and made from wood grown in well-managed forests and other controlled sources. The logging and manufacturing processes are expected to conform to the environmental regulations of the country of origin.

Orders: **Teachers** please contact Bookpoint Ltd, 130 Park Drive, Milton Park, Abingdon, Oxon OX14 4SE. Telephone: (44) 01235 400555. Email primary@bookpoint.co.uk. Lines are open from 9 a.m. to 5 p.m., Monday to Saturday, with a 24-hour message answering service.

Parents, Tutors please call: 020 3122 6405 (Monday to Friday, 9:30 a.m. to 4.30 p.m.). Email: parentenquiries@galorepark.co.uk

Visit our website at www.galorepark.co.uk for details of other revision guides for Common Entrance, examination papers and Galore Park publications.

ISBN: 978 1 510449 71 8

© David E Hanson 2019
First published in 2019 by
Hodder & Stoughton Limited
An Hachette UK Company
Carmelite House
50 Victoria Embankment
London EC4Y 0DZ
www.galorepark.co.uk
Impression number   10 9 8 7 6 5 4 3 2 1
Year   2023 2022 2021 2020 2019

Illustrations by Integra Software Services Pvt. Ltd., Pondicherry, India

Typeset in India
Printed in the UK

A catalogue record for this title is available from the British Library.

Contents and progress record

Section	Page	Length (no. Qs)	Timing (mins)	Question type	Score	Time
Paper 1 Foundation level Representing a CEM test at an average level of challenge for grammar and independent schools.						
Number and calculations	10	20	10	Multiple choice / Standard	/ 20	:
Applying maths	14	14	12	Multiple choice / Standard	/ 14	:
Fractions, proportions and percentages	18	18	14	Multiple choice	/ 18	:
Handling data	22	12	9	Multiple choice	/ 12	:
				Total	/ 64	:
Paper 2 Standard level Representing a CEM test at a medium level of challenge for grammar and independent schools.						
Applying maths	26	18	10	Multiple choice	/ 18	:
Measures, shape and space	29	12	10	Multiple choice / Standard	/ 12	:
Number and calculations	32	16	12	Multiple choice / Standard	/ 16	:
Algebra	35	18	13	Multiple choice	/ 18	:
				Total	/ 64	:
Paper 3 Standard level Representing a CEM test at a medium level of challenge for grammar and independent schools.						
Fractions, proportions and percentages	38	14	6	Multiple choice / Standard	/ 14	:
Handling data	41	16	12	Multiple choice	/ 16	:
Number and calculations	44	12	8	Multiple choice / Standard	/ 12	:
Algebra	47	12	8	Multiple choice	/ 12	:
Applying maths	50	16	11	Multiple choice / Standard	/ 16	:
				Total	/ 70	:

Section	Page	Length (no. Qs)	Timing (mins)	Question type	Score	Time
Paper 4 Advanced level Representing a CEM test at a high level of challenge for grammar and independent schools.						
Number and calculations	54	14	7	Standard	/ 14	:
Measures, shape and space	56	14	11	Standard	/ 14	:
Applying maths	59	16	11	Standard	/ 16	:
Algebra	63	8	5	Standard	/ 8	:
Handling data	64	16	11	Standard	/ 16	:
				Total	/ 68	:

Answers   67

Go to the Galore Park website to download the free PDF answer sheets to use and re-use as many times as you need: galorepark.co.uk/answersheets

How to use this book

Introduction

These practice papers have been written to provide final preparation for your CEM 11+ test, targeting all maths subject areas included as part of the mathematical ability assessments within the CEM 11+ papers. To give you the best chance of success, Galore Park has worked with 11+ tutors, independent schools' teachers, test writers and specialist authors to create these practice papers.

> The actual CEM 11+ test you are going to take will include some or all of these subject areas as well as other small tests covered in the *English*, *Verbal Reasoning* and *Non-Verbal Reasoning Practice Papers* in this series.
>
> Each book concentrates on a single subject so that you can focus your revision on specific skills, brush up on any areas where you may need a little help and then shine in the tests!

This book includes four papers. Each paper is made up of four or five parts, and contains **Number and calculations** and **Applying maths**. Other parts cover **Fractions, proportions and percentages**, **Measures, shape and space**, **Algebra** and **Handling data**.

So that you experience how the CEM tests work, we have included a few key elements to help you become familiar with what to expect:

- Not all of the subject areas will appear in each paper.
- Each test lasts 45 minutes (CEM tests are typically 60 minutes though there are often more questions than you may be able to answer in the time given).
- The sections (or **parts**) within each paper are short and of unpredictable length.
- Each part begins with an untimed introduction and a training question to explain the question format.

The papers increase in difficulty from Paper 1 to Paper 4. This is because CEM tests can change in difficulty both from year to year and from school to school. You will also find that the time allowed for the tests gets shorter to prepare you for the most challenging tests you may face.

It is important to read the instructions carefully as you will be asked to record your answers in a variety of ways:

Separate downloaded answer sheets:

- recording a multiple-choice option on the downloaded multiple-choice answer sheet
- recording the answer on a downloaded number grid.

Recording answers on the paper itself:

- selecting a multiple-choice option, writing the answer letter chosen on the line provided
- writing the answer on the line provided
- choosing an answer from a table and recording your answer on the line provided.

These different styles are included because the online tests expect you to be able to adapt to different recording formats quickly as you move from one part of a paper to the next. These formats can also change from year to year.

As you mark your answers, you will see references to the Galore Park *11+ Mathematics Revision Guide*. These references have been included so that you can go straight to some useful revision tips and find extra practice questions for those areas where you would like more help.

Working through the book

The **Contents and progress record** on pages 3–4 helps you to track your scores and timings as you work through the papers.

You may find some of the questions hard, but don't worry – these tests are designed to make you think. Agree with your parents on a good time to take the test and follow the instructions below to prepare for each paper as if you are actually going to sit your Pre-test/11+ mathematics test.

1 Read the instructions on page 9 before you begin each practice paper.
2 Take the test in a quiet room. Set a timer and record your answers as instructed.
3 Note down how long the test takes you (questions should take an average of about 1 minute each to answer; all questions should be completed even if you run over the time suggested). Aim to complete the paper in the time you are advised. If possible, complete a whole paper in one session.
4 Mark the paper using the answers at the back of the book.
5 Go through the paper again with a friend or parent, talk about the difficult questions and note which parts of the revision guide you are going to review.

The **Answers** can be cut out so that you can mark your papers easily. Do not look at the answers until you have attempted a whole paper.

When you have finished a complete paper, turn back to the **Contents and progress record** and fill in the boxes. Make sure to write your total number of marks and time taken in the **Score** and **Time** boxes.

> If you would like to take further CEM-style papers after completing this book, you will find more papers in the *Pre-test/11+ Mathematics Practice Papers 1 and 2* (see **Continue your learning journey** on page 8).

> **Test day tips**
> Take time to prepare yourself on the day before you go for the test. Remember to take sharpened pencils, an eraser and, if you are allowed, water to maintain your concentration levels and a watch to time yourself.
>
> … and don't forget to have breakfast before you go!

Pre-test and the 11+ entrance exams

This title is part of the Galore Park *Pre-test/11+* series and there are four further *Mathematics Practice Paper* titles (see **Continue your learning journey** on page 8).

This series is designed to help you prepare for Pre-tests and 11+ entrance exams if you are applying to independent schools. These exams are often the same as those set by local grammar schools.

As well as the general CEM test covering more than one subject, Pre-tests and 11+ maths tests appear in a variety of formats and lengths and it is likely that, if you are applying for more than one school, you will encounter more than one of style of test. These include:

● Pre-test/11+ entrance exams in different formats from GL, CEM and ISEB
● Pre-test/11+ entrance exams created specifically for particular schools.

As the tests change all the time it can be difficult to predict the questions, making them harder to revise for. If you are taking more than one style of test, review the books in the **Continue your learning journey** section to see which other titles could be helpful to you.

For parents

For your child to get the maximum benefit from these papers, they should complete them in conditions as close as possible to those they will face in the actual test, as described in the **Working through the book** section on page 6.

Working with your child to follow up the revision work suggested in the answers can improve their performance in areas where they are less confident and boost their chances of success.

For teachers and tutors

The questions become increasingly challenging as the pupils work through these papers to prepare them for the rigours of the CEM tests.

The variety of answer styles is intended to build your pupils' skills in working with different question formats. Some question styles reflect the 'drag and drop' approach of a number of online questions. The standard format test includes questions that require lateral thinking, typical of the most challenging assessments.

Remediation suggested in the answers, referencing the *Revision Guide*, can be helpful for follow-up revision having completed the paper.

Continue your learning journey

When you have completed these *Practice Papers*, you can carry on your learning right up until exam day with the following resources.

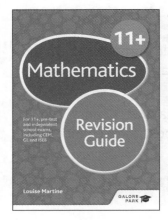  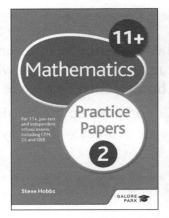 

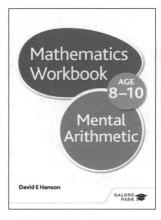 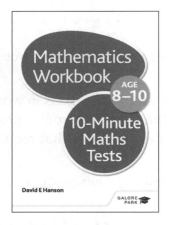 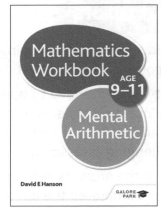 

The *Revision Guide* (referenced in the answers to this book) reviews basic skills in all areas of mathematics, and guidance is provided on how to improve in this subject.

Pre-test/11+ Practice Papers 1 and *2* are designed to provide a complete revision experience across the various test styles you may encounter. Between the two titles there are 13 model papers.

- *Book 1* begins with training tests, and contains a further series of test papers designed to develop your confidence and speed.
- *Book 2* contains GL-style tests and bespoke papers intended for pupils taking the most advanced tests delivered at independent schools.

GL 11+ Mathematics Practice Papers contains four practice papers designed to prepare you for the GL-style tests. Each paper has 50 questions in line with the actual GL test format.

The two *Workbooks* (*Mental Arithmetic Tests* and *10-Minute Maths Tests*) will further develop your skills with 50 mental arithmetic tests and 80 10-minute tests to work through. These titles include more examples of the different types of questions you meet in these *Practice Papers* – the more times you practise answering the questions, the better equipped for the exams you will be.

> Use Atom Learning to improve familiarity with online tests: the online learning platform adapts to your ability to ensure you are always working on your optimal learning path and the adaptive, mock-testing facility looks and scores in the style of the pre-tests.
>
> galorepark.co.uk/atomlearning

Preparing for each paper

Read these instructions before you begin each practice paper.

1 Take the test in a quiet room. Have your timer ready.
2 Check at the beginning of **Part 1** if you will be recording your answers on an **answer sheet**. If a sheet is required, download it from galorepark.co.uk/answersheets and print it out before you begin.
3 The test is made up of either four Parts, 1–4 (Papers 1 and 2) or five Parts, 1–5 (Papers 3 and 4). You should complete all parts of the paper.
4 Each part begins with an introduction and a training question. These pages are untimed and you should read these instructions carefully, then complete the training question before beginning the timed questions.
5 Start the timer *after* completing the introduction to each part and *before* you look at the timed questions.
6 Stop the timer at the end of each part, as instructed.
7 For each Part 1–4 or 1–5:
   a aim for the time given
   b complete all the questions
   c note the actual time you have taken at the end of each part.
8 Answer the questions as described in the introduction at the beginning of each part, using a pencil.
9 If you want to change an answer as you work through a part, rub your answer out and rewrite it. You cannot change an answer after you have completed a part.
10 Work as quickly and efficiently as you can. If a question is difficult to answer, come back to it after finishing the other questions in that part.
11 Aim to answer every question before you finish, even if you are not completely sure of the answer.

Do not look at the answers before completing the entire paper. The instructions in **Working through the book** on page 6 explain how to review your answers.

Always read the instructions on exam papers carefully and make sure you understand exactly what you need to do to answer the questions.

● Paper 1

Download and print the answer sheet from galorepark.co.uk/answersheets before you start this paper.

Complete all four parts of this paper to the timings given at the start of each group of questions. Stop the timer after completing each part and start it again after answering the training question in the next part.

Part 1: Number and calculations

Section time: 10 minutes

How to answer these questions

All your answers to this part should be recorded on the answer sheet you have downloaded.

You will see two types of question:

● Type 1 is multiple choice with answer options A–E.
● Type 2 does not have answer options and your answer is recorded on a number grid.

Look at the examples and then complete the training question. **Do not begin timing yourself until you have finished these pages.**

Example question

Which number is missing from the number sentence below?

$27 - 12 = 22 - \underline{}$

Question type 1: multiple choice

Put a line through the box next to the answer option you have chosen.

7	15	8	12	9
A ▬	B ▢	C ▢	D ▢	E ▢

Answer: **A** 7

$27 - 12 = 15; 22 - 7 = 15$

Question type 2: number grid

Write your answer in the box at the top of the number grid (below) and then put a line through the numbers below. If an answer is a single-digit number, strike through the zero in the tens column.

0	7
0̶	0
1	1
2	2
3	3
4	4
5	5
6	6
7	7̶
8	8
9	9

Now answer the training question.

Training question

Record your answer on the number grid (right),
as shown in the example on the opposite page.

What number is exactly half way between 17 and 107?

0	0
1	1
2	2
3	3
4	4
5	5
6	6
7	7
8	8
9	9

The correct answer is at the bottom of this page.

Use the downloaded answer sheet to record your answers to the questions that follow. You will see the example and training question have already been recorded.

Check your answers only after completing all of Paper 1. The answers are in a cut-out section at the end of the book. Complete the 'results' boxes at the end of this part when you have added up your score. If you run over the time given, complete the questions and note the time you have taken. When you have completed all the questions, record your time in the time box.

Training question answer: 62 $17 + 107 = 124$; $124 \div 2 = 62$; there are other ways.

11

You now have 10 minutes to complete the following 20 questions. Start the timer.

1 What is the total cost of six chocolate bars costing 98 pence each? (1)

£5.94	£5.98	£6.94	£5.96	£5.88
A	B	C	D	E

2 What is the value of $5 \times 7 - 6 \times 3 + 8$? (1)

23	95	$^-31$	48	25
A	B	C	D	E

3 What number is 37 less than 125? (1)

82	92	88	98	86
A	B	C	D	E

4 Which number is closest to 5? (1)

4.9	5.05	4.96	5.1	4.95
A	B	C	D	E

5 What is the number 304.7 written to two significant figures? (1)

300	31	305	30	304
A	B	C	D	E

6 In which number below does the 7 have the greatest value? (1)

7.98	197	7653	96 735	0.078
A	B	C	D	E

7 When the following numbers are arranged in order of size, which will be in the middle? (1)

3.052	3.52	3.502	3.25	3.025
A	B	C	D	E

8 What is the approximate value (to the nearest 100) of the product of 39 and 41? (1)

100	800	1200	1600	8000
A	B	C	D	E

9 What is the product of 23 and 67? (1)

1541	1451	871	335	1311
A	B	C	D	E

10 Amy buys four pens costing 29p each. How much change will she receive from a £5 note? (1)

£3.84	£3.86	£3.76	£3.74	£3.94
A	B	C	D	E

11 Robert has 80 identical bricks with a total mass of 4 kg.
What is the mass of one brick? (1)

5 g	20 g	50 g	200 g	500 g
A	B	C	D	E

12 How many of these numbers are prime? (1)

9   13   41   49   51

1	2	3	4	5
A	B	C	D	E

Training question answer: 44 cm   15 + 7 = 22; 22 × 2 = 44; there are other ways.

12

13 Amber bought three boxes of chocolates each containing 24 chocolates.
   If the total cost was £7.20, what was the cost of each chocolate?   (1)

10p	12p	20p	24p	30p
A	B	C	D	E

14 Mr and Mrs Martin are taking their children to the cinema.
   The cost of each adult ticket is £12, and the cost of each child ticket is £8
   The total cost of the tickets is £56
   How many children are there in the Martin family?   (1)

15 What is the sum of the first five prime numbers?   (1)

16 Which of the following numbers has the largest number of factors?   (1)

            24   25   26   27   28

17 The table shows the numbers of goals scored by the school hockey team.

number of goals	0	1	2	3
number of matches	1	5	4	1

   The team scored two goals in four of their matches.
   What was the total number of goals scored in all of the matches?   (1)

18 What number is exactly half way between 17 and 55?   (1)

19 3 is the first multiple of 3
   How many multiples of 3 are there less than 40?   (1)

20 By how much is 15×7 larger than 17×5?   (1)

Stop the timer. Record your time in the time box below.
Now move on to Part 2.
Record your results for
Part 1 here *after you have*
completed the rest of Paper 1.

Score ☐ /20 Time ☐ : ☐

Part 2: Applying maths

Section time: 12 minutes

How to answer these questions

All your answers to this part should be recorded on the answer sheet you have downloaded.

You will see two types of question:

- Type 1 is multiple choice with answer options A–E.
- Type 2 does not have answer options and your answer is recorded on a number grid.

Look at the examples and then complete the training question. **Do not begin timing yourself until you have finished these pages.**

> ### Example question
> Andy's scores out of ten on five spelling tests were:
>
> 9   6   10   6   7
>
> What was the median score?
>
> **Question type 1: multiple choice**
>
> Put a line through the box next to the answer option you have chosen.
>
> 7   6   8   4   9
>
> A ▬ B ▭ C ▭ D ▭ E ▭
>
> Answer: **A**   7
>
> In order of increasing size, the scores are 6, 6, 7, 9, 10; the median score is the middle one.
>
> **Question type 2: number grid**
>
> Write your answer in the box at the top of the number grid (below) and then put a line through the numbers below. If an answer is a single-digit number, strike through the zero in the tens column.
>
> | 0 | 7 |
> |---|---|
> | 0̶ | 0 |
> | 1 | 1 |
> | 2 | 2 |
> | 3 | 3 |
> | 4 | 4 |
> | 5 | 5 |
> | 6 | 6 |
> | 7 | 7̶ |
> | 8 | 8 |
> | 9 | 9 |

14

Now answer the training question.

Training question

Record your answer on the number grid (right), as shown in the example on the opposite page.

A rectangle is 15 cm long and 7 cm wide.
What is the perimeter of the rectangle?

0	0
1	1
2	2
3	3
4	4
5	5
6	6
7	7
8	8
9	9

The correct answer is at the bottom of this page.

Use the downloaded answer sheet to record your answers to the questions that follow. You will see the examples and training question have already been recorded.

Check your answers only after completing all of Paper 1. The answers are in a cut-out section at the end of the book. Complete the 'results' boxes at the end of this part when you have added up your score. If you run over the time given, complete the questions and note the time you have taken. When you have completed all the questions, record your time in the time box.

Training question answer: **44 cm** $15 \times 2 = 30$; $7 \times 2 = 14$; $30 + 14 = 44$; there are other ways

You now have 12 minutes to complete the following 14 questions. Start the timer.

1 The two-stage function machine below adds 5 to an input and then multiplies by 3

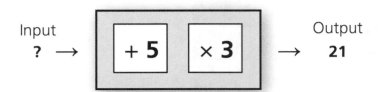

Input
? → [+ 5] [× 3] → Output 21

If the machine output is 21, what was the input?   (1)

1	2	3	4	5
A	B	C	D	E

2 Alice scored the following numbers of rounders in five matches:

4   0   4   0   7

What was the mean (average) number of rounders scored by Alice?   (1)

7	4	3	0	5
A	B	C	D	E

3 Jo bought three CDs costing £4.98 each.

How much change did Jo receive from a £20 note?   (1)

£5.06	£5.03	£6.03	£6.06	£4.97
A	B	C	D	E

4 In a yoga group, three-quarters of the members are female. Seven males are in the group.

How many members are there in the group?   (1)

14	20	21	24	28
A	B	C	D	E

5 John has seven coins worth a total of exactly £1

He has just two types of coin.

What are the two types of coin?   (1)

50p and 5p	20p and 10p	20p and 5p	50p and 10p	50p and 2p
A	B	C	D	E

6 How many of the numbers below are divisible by 6?   (1)

30   612   64   42   126   72   400

2	3	4	5	6
A	B	C	D	E

7 Three number cards are shown below.

The cards can be placed together to make three-digit numbers, for example **497**

4 7 9 → 497

How many different three-digit *odd* numbers, *including 497*, can be made using these cards?   (1)

2	3	4	5	6
A	B	C	D	E

8 The diagram below shows the results when the pupils in a school were asked if they owned a dog.

	boys	girls
own a dog	73	49
do not own a dog	61	88

How many more pupils do *not* own a dog than do own a dog? (1)

14	12	41	24	27
A	B	C	D	E

9 In seven years' time, Sandy will be three times as old as he was a year ago.
How old is Sandy now? (1)

3	4	5	6	7
A	B	C	D	E

10 A farmer has 24 sheep and 16 cows that he needs to move in a trailer.
The trailer can carry up to 7 sheep or up to 3 cows.
The sheep and cows cannot be mixed when being moved.
How many journeys does the cart need to take to move all the sheep and cows? (1)

12	17	20	10	8
A	B	C	D	E

11 Amy has a baking tray that can make 12 muffins at a time.
Amy has an order for 100 muffins.
She fills the baking tray each time before she puts it in the oven, until she has made at least 100 muffins.
How many muffins will she have left over when she has delivered the order of 100? (1)

12 Gita has a favourite single-digit number.
When she squares her number and then subtracts it from the result, she gets 12
What is Gita's favourite number? (1)

13 The grid contains the numbers 1 to 9

4		1	14
		3	14
	2		17
16	17	12	

The row and column totals are printed in white on black.
What number goes in the grey box? (1)

14 The first three patterns in a sequence are shown below.

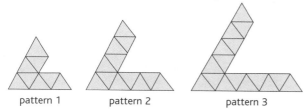

pattern 1   pattern 2   pattern 3

How many small triangles will there be in pattern 6? (1)

Stop the timer. Record your time in the time box below.
Now move on to Part 3.
Record your results for Part 2 here
after you have completed the rest of Paper 1.

Score [   ] /14   Time [   ] : [   ]

Part 3: Fractions, proportions and percentages

How to answer these questions

All your answers to this part should be recorded on the answer sheet you have downloaded.

Look at the example and then complete the training question. **Do not begin timing yourself until you have finished this page.**

> ### Example question
>
> Choose an answer to the question from the choice below. Put a line through the box next to the answer option you have chosen.
>
> What is 24% of 440 kg?
>
> | 110 kg | 105.60 kg | 114.40 g | 104 kg | 114.04 kg |
> |--------|-----------|----------|--------|-----------|
> | A ☐ | B ▬ | C ☐ | D ☐ | E ☐ |
>
> Answer: **B 105.60 kg**
> 25% of 440 kg = 110 kg; 1% of 440 kg = 4.4 kg;
> 110 kg − 4.4 kg = 105.6 kg

Now answer the training question.

> ### Training question
>
> Choose an answer, as shown in the example above.
>
> What is the fraction $\frac{3}{5}$ written as a percentage?
>
> | 12% | 35% | 60% | 53% | 80% |
> |-----|-----|-----|-----|-----|
> | A ☐ | B ☐ | C ☐ | D ☐ | E ☐ |
>
> The correct answer is at the bottom of this page.

Use the downloaded answer sheet to record your answers to the questions that follow. You will see the example and training question have already been recorded.

Check your answers only after completing all of Paper 1. The answers are in a cut-out section at the end of the book. Complete the 'results' boxes at the end of this part when you have added up your score. If you run over the time given, complete the questions and note the time you have taken. When you have completed all the questions, record your time in the time box.

You now have 14 minutes to complete the following 18 questions. Start the timer.

1   What is 25% written as a fraction in its simplest form (lowest terms)?   (1)

$\frac{2}{5}$ $\frac{1}{4}$ $\frac{25}{100}$ $\frac{1}{4}$ $\frac{1}{5}$

A   B   C   D   E

2   At Mallow Farm there are 124 cows and twice as many sheep as cows.

How many animals are there at Mallow Farm?   (1)

372   248   360   166   496

A   B   C   D   E

3   What is 15% of 60?   (1)

9   15   10   6   8

A   B   C   D   E

4   Angel and Bryony share a box of 24 sweets in the ratio 1:3

How many more sweets does Bryony eat than Angel eats?   (1)

8   9   10   11   12

A   B   C   D   E

5   The pictogram below shows the numbers of boys and girls in Year 6.

boys	OOOOOOOO
girls	OOOOOOOOOOOO

One symbol O represents two children.

What is the ratio of the numbers of boys to girls in Year 6, written in its simplest form?   (1)

4:6   2:3   1:2   8:12   16:24

A   B   C   D   E

6   Sean has saved £56 towards a new mobile phone that costs £280

What percentage of the cost has Sean saved?   (1)

20%   56%   36%   25%   28%

A   B   C   D   E

7   What fraction, in its lowest terms, of the regular octagon has been shaded?   (1)

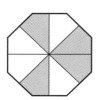

$\frac{4}{8}$ $\frac{4}{9}$ $\frac{1}{2}$ $\frac{3}{8}$ $\frac{1}{3}$

A   B   C   D   E

8   Shobna shared her birthday cake with four friends.
    Shobna had three slices, Wendy had two slices and Vicky, Ulla and Rea each had one slice.
    There were four slices left.
    What fraction of the whole cake did Shobna eat?   (1)

    $\frac{1}{5}$ $\frac{1}{4}$ $\frac{1}{3}$ $\frac{1}{2}$ $\frac{3}{8}$

    A   B   C   D   E

9   A magazine has 60 pages and 18 of the pages are printed in colour.
    What percentage of the pages is printed in colour?   (1)

    20%   30%   18%   36%   28%

    A   B   C   D   E

10 What is a half of one-third?   (1)

    one-quarter   one-third   one-twelfth   one-sixth   two-thirds

    A   B   C   D   E

11 A sweater normally priced at £45 is reduced by 20% in a sale.
    What is the sale price of the sweater?   (1)

    £40   £35   £36   £40.50   £35.50

    A   B   C   D   E

12 Tom and Jerry share a bag of 24 sweets in the ratio 5:7
    How many sweets does Tom get?   (1)

    4   6   8   10   12

    A   B   C   D   E

13 What is the fraction $\frac{4}{5}$ written as a decimal?   (1)

    0.4   0.6   0.45   0.8   0.75

    A   B   C   D   E

14 What is 40% of 300?   (1)

    80   120   12   43   140

    A   B   C   D   E

15 When the following fractions are written in order of size, which will be in the middle?   (1)

    $\frac{4}{9}$ $\frac{1}{2}$ $\frac{3}{8}$ $\frac{3}{2}$ $\frac{3}{4}$

    A   B   C   D   E

16 What is $3 \times 1\frac{3}{4}$?   (1)

    $5\frac{1}{4}$ $4\frac{1}{2}$ $5\frac{3}{4}$ $4\frac{7}{12}$ $5\frac{1}{12}$

    A   B   C   D   E

17 Jack and Jill have buckets with capacities in the ratio 3:2
    They each fill identical barrels with water.
    Jill's barrel is full after she has made 30 trips with her bucket.
    How many trips will Jack make before his barrel is full?   (1)

    60   30   20   25   15

    A   B   C   D   E

18 Amit has eaten one-third of a pizza.

He says that Deepak can eat one-quarter of what is left.

What fraction of the whole pizza will Deepak eat?   (1)

$\frac{1}{5}$	$\frac{2}{5}$	$\frac{1}{12}$	$\frac{1}{6}$	$\frac{5}{6}$
A	B	C	D	E

Stop the timer. Record your time in the time box below.

Now move on to Part 4.

Record your results for Part 3 here
after you have completed the rest of Paper 1.

Score ☐ /18   Time ☐ : ☐

Part 4: Handling data

How to answer these questions

All your answers to this part should be recorded on the answer sheet you have downloaded.

Look at the example and then complete the training question. **Do not begin timing yourself until you have finished this page.**

Example question

Choose an answer to the question from the choice below. Put a line through the box next to the answer option you have chosen.

The masses of John's six dogs are:

20 kg   15 kg   30 kg   25 kg   10 kg   15 kg

What is the range of masses?

30 kg	20 kg	15 kg	25 kg	10 kg
A ▭	B ▬▬	C ▭	D ▭	E ▭

Answer: B 20 kg

The range is the difference between the smallest (10 kg) and largest (30 kg) values; $30 - 10 = 20$

Now answer the training question.

Training question

Choose an answer, as shown in the example above.

The mean mass of five pupils is 48 kg.
What is the total mass of the five pupils?

9.6 kg	230 kg	240 kg	485 kg	548 kg
A ▭	B ▭	C ▭	D ▭	E ▭

The correct answer is at the bottom of this page.

Use the downloaded answer sheet to record your answers to the questions that follow. You will see the example and training question have already been recorded.

Check your answers only after completing all of Paper 1. The answers are in a cut-out section at the end of the book. Complete the 'results' boxes at the end of this part when you have added up your score. If you run over the time given, complete the questions and note the time you have taken. When you have completed all the questions, record your time in the time box.

Training question answer: C 240 kg $5 \times 48 = 240$

You now have 9 minutes to complete the following 12 questions. Start the timer.

1   James has a bag containing the nine coloured balls shown below.

He picks a ball at random from the bag.
What is the likelihood that James will pick a black ball?   (1)

impossible	unlikely	even	likely	certain
A	B	C	D	E

2   The chart below represents the numbers of animals at Dale Farm.

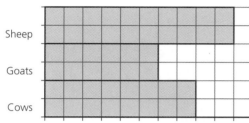

Number of animals

There are six goats at Dale Farm.
What is the total number of animals at Dale Farm?   (1)

18	24	28	36	48
A	B	C	D	E

3   The pupils in a class were asked to choose a favourite 'supper' from the chip shop menu.

	fish	chicken	burger
boys	4	4	5
girls	5	?	6

If there are six more girls in the class than there are boys, how many girls
chose chicken?   (1)

5	6	7	8	9
A	B	C	D	E

4   Reeta tipped the coins out of her purse and drew the bar chart below.

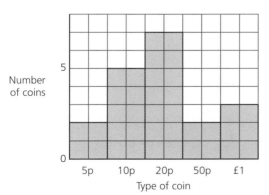

What is the total value of Reeta's coins?   (1)

£5.80	£5.50	£6.00	£5.90	£6.10
A	B	C	D	E

5   The bar chart shows the heights of young plants.

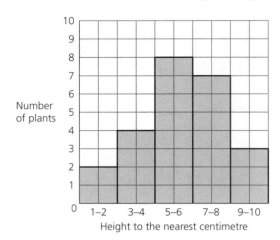

Height to the nearest centimetre

Which statement *must* be true?   (1)

   A   One plant is 1 cm tall.
   B   Three plants are at least 10 cm tall.
   C   One-sixth of the plants are either 3 or 4 cm tall.
   D   Most of the plants are either 5 or 6 cm tall.
   E   There are 20 plants in the study.

6   The table shows the total numbers of sweets eaten by Tamsin in one week.

day	S	M	Tu	W	Th	F	Sa
number of sweets	1	2	5	4	0	2	7

What was the mean (average) number of sweets eaten by Tamsin in a day?   (1)

2	2.5	3	3.5	4
A	B	C	D	E

7   Aadi scored the following numbers of runs in his last eight innings:

     45   78   0   12   23   104   45   39

What was his median score?   (1)

23	45	34	29	42
A	B	C	D	E

8   The pictogram below shows the results of a survey into the numbers of pupils owning dogs and/or cats.

numbers of pupils owning dogs	☺☺☺☺☺☺☺
number of pupils owning cats	☺☺☺☺☺☺☺☺☺

One symbol represents one pupil.
There are 12 pupils in the class and they all own a dog or a cat or both.
How many pupils own both dogs and cats?   (1)

none	2	3	4	6
A	B	C	D	E

9 The table shows the proportions of different types of fruit tree in an orchard.

type of tree	apple	pear	plum	damson
proportion	30%		25%	25%

There are 60 apple trees in the orchard.

How many pear trees are there?   (1)

20	30	40	45	48
A	B	C	D	E

10 The 16 pupils in a class recorded the numbers of brothers and sisters they have.

number of brothers and sisters	number of pupils
0	3
1	5
2	6
3	2

The teacher invites all 16 pupils and all their brothers and sisters to a party.

How many children does the teacher invite to the party?   (1)

22	42	48	39	17
A	B	C	D	E

11 When the spinner is spun, which one of the following statements is true?   (1)

A   The spinner is most likely to land on white.
B   The spinner has a more than even chance of landing on grey.
C   The spinner is as likely to land on white as to land on grey.
D   The spinner is least likely to land on grey.
E   Spun ten times, you would expect it to land on black four times.

12 The range of heights of the pupils in Year 6 is 11.9 cm.

The tallest pupil's height is 143.7 cm.

What is the height of the shortest pupil?   (1)

131.8 cm	130.6 cm	132.8 cm	131.2 cm	155.6 cm
A	B	C	D	E

Stop the timer. Record your time in the time box below.
Record your results for Part 4 here.

Score [   ] / 12   Time [   ] : [   ]

Record your total score and time for Paper 1 here.

Score [   ] / 64   Time [   ] : [   ]

 # Paper 2

Complete all four parts of this paper to the timings given at the start of each set of questions. Stop the timer after completing each part and start it again after answering the training question in the next part.

Part 1: Applying maths

Section time: 10 minutes

How to answer these questions

All your answers to this part should be recorded on this paper.

Look at the example and then complete the training question. **Do not begin timing yourself until you have finished this page.**

> ### Example question
>
> Choose an answer to the question from the table below. Write the letter of the answer you have chosen on the answer line provided.
>
> The three digits 4, 5 and 6 can be arranged to make 3-digit numbers, such as 654 (the largest).
> How many other 3-digit numbers (*not counting 654*) can be made using the digits 4, 5 and 6?
> Answer: __H__   5
> The other numbers in order are 456, 465, 546, 564, 645
> Making an organised list is helpful.

Now answer the training question.

> ### Training question
>
> Choose an answer to the question from the table below and record your answer, as shown in the example above. No answer can be used more than once (so you cannot choose option **H**).
>
> How many multiples of 5 are there less than 99? _____
> The correct answer is at the bottom of this page.

A 50	B 60	C 0	D 206.2	E 33.5
F 30 + 5	G 7:9	H 5	I 19	J 6
K 5 + (−10)	L −45	M 7:2	N −5	O 19
P 3.7	Q 74	R 17.5	S 3:6	T 2760

Record your answers to the questions that follow on the lines provided. No option can be used more than once.

Check your answers only after completing all of Paper 2. The answers are in a cut-out section at the end of the book. Complete the 'results' boxes at the end of this part when you have added up your score. If you run over the time given, complete the questions and note the time you have taken. When you have completed all the questions, record your time in the time box.

You now have 10 minutes to complete the following 18 questions. Start the timer.

Choose your answers to questions 1 to 9 from the table below. No option can be used more than once.

A 11.7	B $\frac{4}{9}$	C $\frac{1}{2}$	D 153.01	E 20%
F 53	G $\frac{1}{4}$	H 151.03	I $\frac{3}{4}$	J 10.71
K $\frac{2}{3}$	L 149.31	M 80%	N 10.70	O 11.8
P £46.38	Q 76	R 52	S £43.68	T $\frac{1}{3}$

1   Morgan's calculator display shows the number

10.70485

What is this number written to two decimal places? _____ (1)

2   What number is 17.46 smaller than 166.77? _____ (1)

3   Mandy bought a sweater originally priced at £36 for £28.80 in a sale.

What was the percentage reduction in the sale? _____ (1)

4   The runners in a 4×100 metres relay race finish in a total time of 46.8 seconds.

What is the average time for a runner to complete his 100 metres? _____ seconds (1)

5   Lucy leaves school at 15:45 and arrives home at 16:38

How many minutes does her journey take? _____ minutes (1)

6   Vijay eats one-quarter of his birthday cake and gives Amy one-third of what is left.

What fraction of the whole cake does Amy eat? _____ (1)

7   Romilly gets 80p pocket money every week. In December, she is awarded a 5% increase for the following year.

How much money will she receive in total next year (52 weeks)? _____ (1)

8   Tom has £3.60 and loses coins of value £1.60

What fraction (in its lowest terms) of the money has Tom lost? _____ (1)

9   It is seven weeks and three days until Mary's birthday.

How many days is that? _____ days (1)

Choose your answers to questions 10 to 18 from the table below. No option can be used more than once.

A 87	B 1	C 17	D 12	E 83
F 30	G 7	H 32	I 180	J 85
K 9	L 270	M 57	N 2	O 4
P 112	Q 10	R 26	S 16	T 36

10 What is the sum of all the prime numbers between 10 and 30? _____ (1)

11 To calculate the number of sandwiches, n, needed for a picnic, Clare uses the formula $n = 4a + 2c + 6$, where a is the number of adults and c is the number of children.
How many sandwiches are needed for three adults and seven children? _____ (1)

12 Three consecutive *even* integers (whole numbers) have a sum of 102
What is the largest of the three numbers? _____ (1)

13 In a school of 450 pupils, 40% are boys.
How many girls are there? _____ (1)

14 Ahmed has £11.40 in 20p coins.
How many 20p coins does he have? _____ (1)

15 How many of the following numbers are divisible by 3? _____
24   33   53   69   102   1033 (1)

16 64 is a square number (8^2) and a cube number (4^3).
What other number less than 100 is both a square number and a cube number? _____ (1)

17 Will has a favourite number. When he adds 4, then multiplies by 3 and finally subtracts 7, he gets 26
What is Will's favourite number? _____ (1)

18 What is the missing number in this sequence? _____
2   3   7   23   ...   343   1367 (1)

Stop the timer. Record your time in the time box below.
Now move on to Part 2.
Record your results for Part 1 here *after you have completed the rest of Paper 2.*

Score [ ] /18   Time [ ] : [ ]

Part 2: Measures, shape and space

Section time: 10 minutes

How to answer these questions

All your answers to this part should be recorded on this paper.

You will see two types of question:

- Type 1 is multiple choice with answer options A–E.

- Type 2 does not have answer options.

Look at the examples and then complete the training question. **Do not begin timing yourself until you have finished this page.**

Example question

A garden store in the shape of a cuboid has a length of 6 m, a width of 5 m and a volume of 240 m³.

What is its depth?

Question type 1: multiple choice
Write the letter of the answer you have chosen on the line provided.

6 m	7 m	8 m	9 m	10 m
A	B	C	D	E

Answer: __C__   **8 m**

$6 m \times 5 m = 30 m^2$; $240 m^3 \div 30 m^2 = 8 m$

Question type 2: standard
Write your answer on the line provided.
Answer: __8__

Now answer the training question.

Training question

Write the letter of the answer you have chosen on the line provided, as shown in the example above.

A box in the shape of a cuboid has a length of 30 cm, a width of 20 cm and a volume of 3000 cm³. What is its depth?

3 cm	5 cm	10 cm	12 cm	1 m
A	B	C	D	E

The correct answer is at the bottom of this page. _____

Record your answers to the questions that follow on the lines provided.

Check your answers only after completing all of Paper 2. The answers are in a cut-out section at the end of the book. Complete the 'results' boxes at the end of this part when you have added up your score. If you run over the time given, complete the questions and note the time you have taken. When you have completed all the questions, record your time in the time box.

Training question answer: **B 5 cm** $30 cm \times 20 cm = 600 cm^2$; $3000 cm^3 \div 600 cm^2 = 5 cm$

You now have 10 minutes to complete the following 12 questions. Start the timer.

1   In Madrid, the temperature is 33 °C.
    In Paris, the temperature is 19 °C.
    How many degrees warmer is it in Madrid than in Paris?   (1)

13°	14°	16°	24°	26°
A	B	C	D	E	_____

2   What is the area of the shape?   (1)

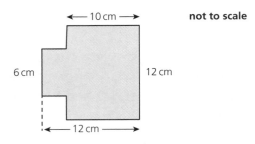

124 cm²	132 cm²	138 cm²	140 cm²	144 cm²
A	B	C	D	E	_____

3   How many of the shapes below have *one and only one* line of symmetry?   (1)

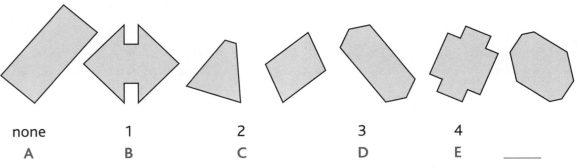

none	1	2	3	4
A	B	C	D	E	_____

4   A piece of wire is bent to form a regular hexagon with sides of length 8 cm.

The wire is straightened out and then bent again to form a square.
What is the length of a side of the square?   (1)

8 cm	10 cm	12 cm	14 cm	16 cm
A	B	C	D	E	_____

5   Carole's snake is 8 feet 6 inches long. Assume that one foot is the same as 30 cm.
    What is the length of the snake in centimetres?   (1)

240 cm	250 cm	255 cm	260 cm	270 cm
A	B	C	D	E	_____

Questions 6 to 8 are concerned with the measuring containers P and Q below, containing lemonade.

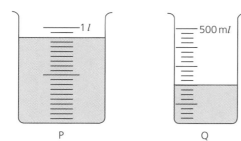

6   The volume of lemonade in container P is 900 ml.
    Write this as a fraction of a litre in its simplest form (lowest terms).

    _____ litre   (1)

7   What is the volume of lemonade, *in litres*, in container Q?

    Give your answer as a decimal. _____ litre   (1)

8   How many 150 ml glasses could be filled with the lemonade in container P?

    _____ glasses   (1)

Questions 9 to 12 are concerned with the two triangles in the diagram below.

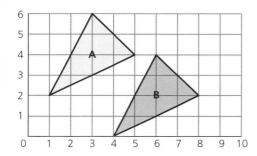

9   What type of triangles are these? _____   (1)

10 What is the area (in square units) of one triangle? _____ units²   (1)

11 What word describes the transformation that would map triangle A onto

    triangle B? _____   (1)

12 What are the co-ordinates of the vertex (corner) of triangle A that is closest

    to triangle B? (_____ , _____)   (1)

Stop the timer. Record your time in the time box below.
Now move on to Part 3.
Record your results for Part 2 here *after* you have completed the rest of Paper 2.

Part 3: Number and calculations

How to answer these questions

All your answers to this part should be recorded on this paper.

You will see two types of question:

- Type 1 is multiple choice with answer options A–E.
- Type 2 does not have answer options.

Look at the examples and then complete the training question. **Do not begin timing yourself until you have finished this page.**

Example question

Tom and Jerry share 12 sweets in the ratio 3 : 1
How many more sweets does Tom get than Jerry gets?

Question type 1: multiple choice
Write the letter of the answer you have chosen on the line provided.

2	3	4	5	6
A	B	C	D	E

Answer: __E__ 6

There are four shares (3 + 1); there are three sweets in each share (12 ÷ 4); Tom gets three shares, so he gets 9 (3 × 3) sweets and Jerry gets one share of three sweets; Tom gets six more sweets than Jerry (9 − 3 = 6).

Question type 2: standard
Write your answer on the line provided.

6 __E__

Now answer the training question.

Training question

Write the letter beneath the answer you have chosen on the line provided, as shown in the example above.

Jack and Jill share 20 sweets in the ratio 2 : 3
How many sweets does Jill get?

8	9	10	12	15	
A	B	C	D	E	_____

The correct answer is at the bottom of this page.

Record your answers to the questions that follow on the lines provided.

Check your answers only after completing all of Paper 2. The answers are in a cut-out section at the end of the book. Complete the 'results' boxes at the end of this part when you have added up your score. If you run over the time given, complete the questions and note the time you have taken. When you have completed all the questions, record your time in the time box.

Training question answer: **D** 12   There are five shares (2 + 3 = 5); there are four sweets in each share (20 ÷ 5 = 4); Jill gets three shares, so she gets 12 (3 × 4 = 12) sweets.

You now have 12 minutes to complete the following 16 questions. Start the timer.

1   The diagram shows part of a jumbled multiplication square.

×	7	5	8	6
9	63	45	72	54
3	21	15		18
8		15	64	48
3	28	20	32	24

Which two numbers are missing?   (1)

24, 63	56, 24	63, 32	56, 32	24, 48
A	B	C	D	E	_____

2   What is the next number in this sequence?   (1)

$$1 \quad 5 \quad 13 \quad 29 \quad ...$$

61	58	63	71	68
A	B	C	D	E	_____

3   Which of the following numbers is a multiple of both 7 and 5?   (1)

75	140	57	95	215
A	B	C	D	E	_____

4   Colin and Lisa share 40 sweets in the ratio 3 : 5

How many more sweets does Lisa get than Colin gets?   (1)

8	10	12	15	18
A	B	C	D	E	_____

5   Rona multiplied her favourite number by 5, then subtracted 5 and finally multiplied by 3

The result was 60

What is Rona's favourite number?   (1)

3	4	5	6	7
A	B	C	D	E	_____

6   What is the value of 3^4?   (1)

12	64	27	81	34
A	B	C	D	E	_____

7   How many of these numbers are prime?   (1)

$$2 \quad 9 \quad 13 \quad 41 \quad 49 \quad 51$$

1	2	3	4	5
A	B	C	D	E	_____

8   Findlay has identical wooden cubes, each one with an edge length of 28 mm.
He places cubes on top of each other until the pile is just over 30 cm high.   (1)
How many cubes are in the pile? _____ cubes

9   What is the smallest answer given by one of these calculations?   (1)
$(5 + 4) \times 3 - 2 =$ $5 + (4 \times 3) - 2 =$ $5 + 4 \times 3 - 2 =$ $5 + 4 \times (3 - 2) =$ _____

10   The sum of two prime numbers is 54 and the difference between them is 20   (1)
What is the larger of the two prime numbers? _____

11 What is the product of 11 and 13? _____ (1)

12 Jasmine bought some cereal bars costing 64 pence each.
   She received £5.52 in change from a £10 note.
   How many cereal bars did she buy? _____ (1)

13 What is the smallest number that is divisible by both 9 and 12? _____ (1)

14 The machine subtracts 2 and then multiplies by 3

Input
10 → [−2] [×3] → Output ?

   When 10 is put in, what number comes out? _____ (1)

15 What is the number **53.545** written to the nearest tenth? _____ (1)

16 What is one-quarter of one-third of 90? _____ (1)

Stop the timer. Record your time in the time box below.
Now move on to Part 4.
Record your results for Part 3 here *after*
you have completed the rest of Paper 2.

Score [   ] /16 Time [   ] : [   ]

Part 4: Algebra

How to answer these questions

All your answers to this part should be recorded on this paper.

Look at the example and then complete the training question. **Do not begin timing yourself until you have finished this page.**

> ### Example question
> Choose an answer to the question from the table below. Write the letter of the answer you have chosen on the answer line provided.
> Simplify, as far as possible, the expression $3a + 4a - 5a$
> Answer: **B 2a**
> $3a + 4a = 7a$ and then $7a - 5a = 2a$; remember that $3a$ means $3 \times a$

Now answer the training question.

> ### Training question
> Choose an answer to the question from the table below and record your answer, as shown in the example above. No answer can be used more than once (so you cannot choose option B).
>
> Simplify, as far as possible, the expression $3a - 2b + 4a + 5b$ _____
> The correct answer is at the bottom of this page.

A $3a$	B $2a$	C $b-a$	D $5b$	E $4a+3b$
F $a+b$	G $7a-3b$	H $3a+7b$	I $3a-7b$	J $5ab$
K $2a-b$	L $-2a$	M $2ab$	N $7a+3b$	O $10ab$
P $5b$	Q $7a$	R $2a+3$	S a	T $12a$

Record your answers to the questions that follow on the lines provided. No option can be used more than once.

Check your answers only after completing all of Paper 2. The answers are in a cut-out section at the end of the book. Complete the 'results' boxes at the end of this part when you have added up your score. If you run over the time given, complete the questions and note the time you have taken. When you have completed all the questions, record your time in the time box.

Training question answer: **N $7a + 3b$** $3a + 4a = 7a$ and $5b - 2b = 3b$ (we 'collect' like terms)

Choose your answer to questions 1 to 9 from the table below. No option can be used more than once.

A ×	B 17	C 2p − 3	D ÷	E n + 17
F 2p + 3	G 7xy	H 4x + 3y	I 17 − n	J 5
K n − 17	L 16	M +	N 3x + 4y	O 10
P 19	Q −	R 23p	S −1	T 8

You now have 13 minutes to complete the following 18 questions. Start the timer.

1   In the statement below, the box represents an operation (+ − × or ÷).

   39 ☐ 3 = 13

   Which operation should be in the box? _____ (1)

2   The symbol ⓪ represents a number.

   ⓪ + ⓪ = 32

   What is the number ⓪? _____ (1)

3   The machine multiplies by 2 and then adds 3

   Input p → | × 2 | + 3 | → Output ?

   When p is put in, what comes out? _____ (1)

4   An orange costs x pence and a pear costs y pence.

   What is the cost, in pence, of four oranges and three pears? _____ (1)

5   Neil's older sister Amelia was n years old when Neil was born.

   Amelia is now 17 years old. How old is Neil? _____ (1)

6   What is the value of the expression 4a − 3b when a is 5 and b is 7? _____ (1)

7   Two numbers p and q have a sum of 14 and a difference of 2

   What is the larger number? _____ (1)

8   The symbols # and @ represent two integers (whole numbers).

   @ × # = 60 and @ − # = 7

   What is the value of @ + # ? _____ (1)

9   What is the missing number in the sequence below? _____

   1   7   13   ...   25 (1)

Choose your answers to questions 10 to 18 from the table below. No option may be used more than once.

A 1	B 6	C 13	D 5	E 28
F 2	G 36	H 33	I 21	J 9
K 17	L 4	M 12	N 3	O 10
P 11	Q 7	R 8	S 11	T 23

For each of questions 10 to 14, solve the equation to find the value of *a*.

10 $a + 3 = 9$ _____ (1)

11 $a - 3 = 9$ _____ (1)

12 $3a + 3 = 18$ _____ (1)

13 $2a - 3 = 15$ _____ (1)

14 $2(2a + 3) = 22$ _____ (1)

Questions 15 to 18 are concerned with the patterns below.

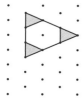 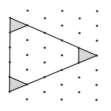 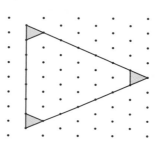

pattern 1
side length 3 units
perimeter 9 units
1 dot inside

pattern 2
side length 5 units
perimeter 15 units
6 dots inside

pattern 3
side length 7 units

15 How many shaded triangles will there be in pattern 5? _____ (1)

16 What is the side length of pattern 6? _____ (1)

17 What is the perimeter (in units) of pattern 5? _____ (1)

18 How many dots are there *inside* the white hexagon in pattern 4? _____ (1)

Stop the timer. Record your time in the time box below.
Record your results for Part 4 here.

Score [   ] /18 Time [   ] : [   ]

Record your total score and time for Paper 2 here.

Score [   ] /64 Time [   ] : [   ]

● Paper 3

Download and print the answer sheet from galorepark.co.uk/answersheets before you start this paper.

Complete all four parts of this paper to the timings given at the start of each set of questions. Stop the timer after completing each part and start it again after answering the training question in the next part.

Part 1: Fractions, proportions and percentages

Section time: 6 minutes

How to answer these questions

All your answers to this part should be recorded on the answer sheet you have downloaded.

You will see two types of question:

● Type 1 is multiple choice with answer options A–E.
● Type 2 does not have answer options and your answer is recorded on a number grid.

Look at the examples and then complete the training question. **Do not begin timing yourself until you have finished these pages.**

Example questions

Question type 1: multiple choice

Put a line through the box next to the answer option you have chosen.

What is the fraction $\frac{24}{36}$ written in the simplest form (lowest terms)?

$\frac{2}{3}$ $\frac{3}{4}$ $\frac{6}{9}$ $\frac{12}{18}$ $\frac{8}{12}$
A ▬ B ☐ C ☐ D ☐ E ☐

Answer: A $\frac{2}{3}$

Both numerator (24) and denominator (36) of $\frac{24}{36}$ divide by 12

Question type 2: number grid

Write your answer in the box at the top of the number grid (below) and then put a line through the numbers below. If an answer is a single-digit number, strike through the zero in the tens column. What is 20% of 35?

0	7
0̶	0
1	1
2	2
3	3
4	4
5	5
6	6
7	7̶
8	8
9	9

Answer: **7**

There are several ways: 20% is the same as $\frac{1}{5}$ so $35 \div 5 = 7$; 10% of 35 is 3.5, so 20% is 3.5×2

Now answer the training question.

Training question

Record your answer on the number grid (right), as shown in the example on the opposite page.

What is 40% of 120?

0	0
1	1
2	2
3	3
4	4
5	5
6	6
7	7
8	8
9	9

The correct answer is at the bottom of this page.

Use the downloaded answer sheet to record your answers to the questions that follow. You will see the examples and training question have already been recorded.

Check your answers only after completing all of Paper 3. The answers are in a cut-out section at the end of the book. Complete the 'results' boxes at the end of this part when you have added up your score. If you run over the time given, complete the questions and note the time you have taken. When you have completed all the questions, record your time in the time box.

You now have 6 minutes to complete the following 14 questions. Start the timer.

1 When the following numbers are written in order of size, which will be in the middle? (1)

49.3	50.1	49.9	48.9	49.8
A	B	C	D	E

2 What is the fraction seven-eighths written as a decimal? (1)

0.87	0.885	0.78	0.785	0.875
A	B	C	D	E

3 What is two-thirds of $4\frac{1}{2}$? (1)

$3\frac{1}{2}$	3	$2\frac{3}{4}$	$2\frac{1}{3}$	$2\frac{2}{3}$
A	B	C	D	E

4 In a group of 60 children, 24 are boys. What percentage of the group are girls? (1)

32%	36%	60%	72%	40%
A	B	C	D	E

5 What score out of 20 gives a percentage of 70%? (1)

6 What is 39.48 written to two significant figures? (1)

7 40% of the 120 pupils in Year 6 own dogs. How many pupils do *not* own dogs? (1)

8 Naga and Saima share 50 sweets in the ratio 3:7
How many sweets does Naga get? (1)

9 What is one-third of 243? (1)

10 220 grams of fruit cocktail will serve two people. How many grams of fruit cocktail are needed for a party of seven people? (1)

11 What is $3\frac{1}{2}$% of 1000? (1)

12 By how much is one-eighth of 400 less than one-sixth of 360? (1)

13 What is $3\frac{2}{3} + 2\frac{1}{4} + 1\frac{3}{4} + 5\frac{1}{3}$? (1)

14 On this test of 14 questions, Ava's score was converted to a percentage. To the nearest 1%, Ava's percentage was recorded as 64%. How many of the 14 questions did Ava get right? (1)

Stop the timer. Record your time in the time box below.
Now move on to Part 2.

Record your results for Part 1 here *after you have completed the rest of Paper 3.*

Score ☐ /14 Time ☐ : ☐

Part 2: Handling data

How to answer these questions

All your answers to this part should be recorded on the answer sheet you have downloaded.

Look at the example and then complete the training question. **Do not begin timing yourself until you have finished this page.**

Example question

Choose an answer to the question from the choices below. Put a line through the box next to the answer option you have chosen.

Tommy's scores on five mental arithmetic tests were:

| 14 | 18 | 13 | 19 | 16 |

What was Tommy's mean score?

| 14 | 14.5 | 15 | 15.5 | 16 |
| A ☐ | B ☐ | C ☐ | D ☐ | E ▬ |

Answer: **E 16**

The sum of the scores is 80 (14 + 18 + 13 + 19 + 16); 80 ÷ 5 = 16

Now answer the training question.

Training question

Choose an answer, as shown in the example above.

For four numbers, the mean is 5, the median is 5, the mode is 5 and the range is 6
What is the largest of the four numbers?

| 6 | 7 | 8 | 9 | 10 |
| A | B | C | D | E |

The correct answer is at the bottom of this page.

Use the downloaded answer sheet to record your answers to the questions that follow. You will see the example and training question have already been recorded.

Check your answers only after completing all of Paper 3. The answers are in a cut-out section at the end of the book. Complete the 'results' boxes at the end of this part when you have added up your score. If you run over the time given, complete the questions and note the time you have taken. When you have completed all the questions, record your time in the time box.

You now have 12 minutes to complete the following 16 questions. Start the timer.

Questions 1 to 4 are concerned with the Carroll diagram below, which gives details of the sports played by the pupils in Year 6.

	play tennis	do not play tennis
play hockey	17	7
do not play hockey	15	11

1 How many pupils are there in Year 6? (1)

48	49	50	51	52
A	B	C	D	E

2 How many of the pupils play tennis? (1)

32	24	18	34	26
A	B	C	D	E

3 What percentage of the pupils in Year 6 do not play either tennis or hockey? (1)

11%	22%	44%	26%	52%
A	B	C	D	E

4 How many more pupils play tennis than play hockey? (1)

5	6	7	8	9
A	B	C	D	E

Questions 5 to 8 are concerned with the frequency diagram below, which shows the number of goals scored in Terriers' matches last season.

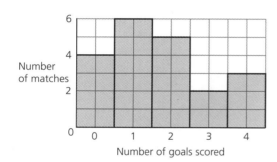

5 How many matches did Terriers play last season? (1)

20	4	10	16	40
A	B	C	D	E

6 How many goals were scored last season? (1)

38	34	20	36	40
A	B	C	D	E

7 What was the modal number of goals scored in a match? (1)

0	1	2	3	4
A	B	C	D	E

8 What was the median number of goals scored in a match? (1)

1	1.5	1.7	2	2.2
A	B	C	D	E

Questions 9 to 12 are concerned with the Zara's counters, shown below.

9 What fraction of Zara's counters are black? (1)

$\frac{1}{2}$ $\frac{1}{3}$ $\frac{3}{10}$ $\frac{3}{8}$ $\frac{2}{3}$

A B C D E

10 What is the ratio of grey:white counters? (1)

1:2 4:3 2:1 4:1 3:1

A B C D E

11 Zara puts the counters in her pocket and then picks one counter at random. What is the probability that she will *not* pick a grey counter? (1)

$\frac{1}{2}$ $\frac{2}{5}$ $\frac{4}{9}$ $\frac{1}{3}$ $\frac{5}{9}$

A B C D E

12 Zara puts back the counter she picked from her pocket. She loses one white counter and cannot find it. She picks, at random, one of the remaining counters from her pocket. What is the probability that the counter picked is black? (1)

$\frac{1}{2}$ $\frac{1}{4}$ $\frac{3}{8}$ $\frac{3}{4}$ $\frac{5}{8}$

A B C D E

Questions 13 to 16 are concerned with the table of data prepared by six friends.

name	age (Y:M)	mass (kg)	height (m)	eye colour
Alice	10:7	45	1.48	blue
Ben	10:6	39	1.37	brown
Clare	10:9	40	1.54	blue
David	11:0	41	1.49	green
Emily	10:5	38	1.62	blue
Flora	10:8	44	1.47	brown

13 Who is 2 kg heavier than Ben? (1)

Alice Ben Clare David Emily

A B C D E

14 When the friends line up in order of height, which *two* will be either side of Flora? *Draw lines in two boxes.* (1)

Alice Ben Clare David Emily

A B C D E

15 Which friend with blue eyes is older than Flora? (1)

Alice Ben Clare David Emily

A B C D E

16 Which *two* friends have a combined mass of 83 kg? *Draw lines in two boxes.* (1)

Alice Ben Clare David Emily

A B C D E

Stop the timer. Record your time in the time box below.
Now move on to Part 3.

Record your results for Part 2 here *after you have completed the rest of Paper 3.*

Score [ ] /16 Time [ ]:[ ]

Part 3: Number and calculations

How to answer these questions

All your answers to this part should be recorded on the answer sheet you have downloaded.

You will see two types of question:

- Type 1 is multiple choice with answer options A–E.
- Type 2 does not have answer options and your answer is recorded on a number grid.

Look at the examples and then complete the training question. **Do not begin timing yourself until you have finished these pages.**

Example question

What is the sum of the first five square numbers?

Question type 1: multiple choice

Put a line through the box next to the answer option you have chosen.

54	29	55	66	75
A ☐	B ☐	C ▬	D ☐	E ☐

Answer: **C 55**

$1^2 + 2^2 + 3^2 + 4^2 + 5^2 =$
$1 + 4 + 9 + 16 + 25 = 55$

Question type 2: number grid

Write your answer in the box at the top of the number grid (below) and then put a line through the numbers below. If an answer is a single-digit number, strike through the zero in the tens column.

5	5
0	0
1	1
2	2
3	3
4	4
5̶	5̶
6	6
7	7
8	8
9	9

Now answer the training question.

Training question

Record your answer on the number grid (right), as shown in the example above.

Two prime numbers have a sum of 63

What is the larger number?

0	0
1	1
2	2
3	3
4	4
5	5
6	6
7	7
8	8
9	9

The correct answer is at the bottom of this page.

Training question answer: 61   One number must be 2 since the total is odd! 63 − 2 = 61

Use the downloaded answer sheet to record your answers to the questions that follow. You will see the examples and training question have already been recorded.

Check your answers only after completing all of Paper 3. The answers are in a cut-out section at the end of the book. Complete the 'results' boxes at the end of this part when you have added up your score. If you run over the time given, complete the questions and note the time you have taken. When you have completed all the questions, record your time in the time box.

You now have 8 minutes to complete the following 12 questions. Start the timer.

1 Which of the following numbers is *not* a prime number? (1)

31	41	51	61	71
A	B	C	D	E

2 Which of the following calculations gives the largest answer? (1)

$256 \div 8$	6^2	5×7	$\sqrt{400}$	$21 + 16$
A	B	C	D	E

3 What is the largest number that will divide exactly into both 80 and 64? (1)

4	16	8	2	18
A	B	C	D	E

4 What is the smallest number that can be divided by both 14 and 21? (1)

420	84	210	42	126
A	B	C	D	E

5 By how much is the product of 11 and 12 greater than the sum of 11 and 12? (1)

6 How many chocolate bars priced at 45p each could you buy for £20? (1)

7 What number is represented by the black square in this statement?

$3 \times (7-2) + 24 \div 6 = 5^2 - 2^3 + \blacksquare$ (1)

Questions 8 to 12 are concerned with the number cards shown below.

| 2 | 0 | 7 | 4 | 9 | 5 |

The cards can be placed side by side to make 2-digit and 3-digit numbers like this:

| 2 | 5 | 4 | → | 2 | 5 | 4 |

8 What is the number closest to 500 that can be made using these cards? (1)

9 What is the largest 2-digit multiple of 3 that can be made? (1)

10 What is the smallest 2-digit prime number that can be made? (1)

11 What is the only 2-digit cube number that can be made? (1)

12 What is the largest factor of 500 that can be made? (1)

Stop the timer. Record your time in the time box below.

Now move on to Part 4.

Record your results for Part 3 here *after* you have completed the rest of Paper 3.

Score ☐ /12   Time ☐ : ☐

Part 4: Algebra

How to answer these questions

All your answers to this part should be recorded on the answer sheet you have downloaded.

Look at the example and then complete the training question. **Do not begin timing yourself until you have finished this page.**

> ### Example question
>
> Choose an answer to the question from the choices below. Put a line through the box next to the answer option you have chosen.
>
> Which of the following is *not* equal to the others?
>
> | $6a + 4b$ | $2(3a + 2b)$ | $4b + 6a$ | $10ab$ | $8a + 4b - 2a$ |
> |-----------|--------------|-----------|--------|----------------|
> | A ⬜ | B ⬜ | C ⬜ | D ▬ | E ⬜ |
>
> Answer: **D 10ab**
>
> The expression $10ab$ involves the product of a and b.

Now answer the training question.

> ### Training question
>
> Choose an answer, as shown in the example above.
>
> Simplify, as far as possible, $2(a + 2b) + 5a - 3b$
>
> | $7a - b$ | $9a + b$ | $7a + b$ | $3a + 7b$ | $7a - 5b$ |
> |----------|----------|----------|-----------|-----------|
> | A | B | C | D | E |
>
> The correct answer is at the bottom of this page.

Use the downloaded answer sheet to record your answers to the questions that follow. You will see the example and training question have already been recorded.

Check your answers only after completing all of Paper 3. The answers are in a cut-out section at the end of the book. Complete the 'results' boxes at the end of this part when you have added up your score. If you run over the time given, complete the questions and note the time you have taken. When you have completed all the questions, record your time in the time box.

Training question answer: **C 7$a + b$** $2(a + 2b) = 2a + 4b$; then $2a + 5a = 7a$ and $4b - 3b = b$

You now have 8 minutes to complete the following 12 questions. Start the timer.

1 Mia has a favourite number. When she adds 4 to her number, then multiplies by 7 and finally subtracts 5, she gets 58
   What is Mia's favourite number? (1)

5	6	7	8	9
A	B	C	D	E

2 Gemma has a favourite number. When she squares her number, then subtracts 12, she gets 4
   What is Gemma's favourite number? (1)

4	5	6	7	8
A	B	C	D	E

3 Alyssa has a favourite number. When she multiplies it by 5 and then subtracts 12, she gets her favourite number! What is Alyssa's favourite number? (1)

2	3	4	5	6
A	B	C	D	E

4 Two numbers p and q are such that $p + q = 15$ and $p - q = 7$
   What number is p? (1)

7	8	9	10	11
A	B	C	D	E

For each of questions 5 to 10, solve the equation to find the value of the unknown number.

5 $4a = 2$ What is a? (1)

2	−2	$\frac{1}{2}$	$-\frac{1}{2}$	8
A	B	C	D	E

6 $3(b + 4) = 18$ What is b? (1)

2	3	4	8	5
A	B	C	D	E

7 $5c - 6 = c + 6$ What is c? (1)

0	1	2	3	4
A	B	C	D	E

8 $2(2d - 8) = 4$ What is d? (1)

1	2	3	4	5
A	B	C	D	E

9 $\frac{e}{4} = 12$ What is e? (1)

3	12	16	48	8
A	B	C	D	E

10 $3(2f - 6) = 2(f + 3)$ What is f? (1)

2	4	5	6	8
A	B	C	D	E

For each of questions 11 and 12, find the number represented by the symbol #.

11 $2\# + 3@ = 17$ and $\# + @ = 7$ (1)

1	2	3	4	5
A	B	C	D	E

12 $\#@ = 24$ and $\frac{\#}{@} = 1\frac{1}{2}$ (1)

2	3	4	5	6
A	B	C	D	E

Stop the timer. Record your time in the time box below.
Now move on to Part 5.

Record your results for Part 4 here *after*
you have completed the rest of Paper 3.

Score ☐ /12 Time ☐ : ☐

Part 5: Applying maths

How to answer these questions

All your answers to this part should be recorded on the answer sheet you have downloaded.

You will see two types of question:

- Type 1 is multiple choice with answer options A–E.
- Type 2 does not have answer options and your answer is recorded on a number grid.

Look at the examples and then complete the training question. **Do not begin timing yourself until you have finished these pages.**

Example questions

Question type 1: multiple choice

Put a line through the box next to the answer option you have chosen.

Tom buys seven packets of sweets priced at 89p each.

How much change does he get from a £10 note?

£3.77　£3.67　£6.63　£3.97　£6.73

A ▭　B ▭　C ▭　D ▭　E ▭

Answer: **A £3.77**

He spends £6.23 (7p less than £6.30 – that is 7p less than $7 \times 90p$); £10.00 − £6.23 = £3.77

Question type 2: number grid

Write your answer in the box at the top of the number grid (below) and then put a line through the numbers below. If an answer is a single-digit number, strike through the zero in the tens column.

Priya buys some packs of sweets costing 89p each.

She gets £2.20 change from a £20 note.

How many packs of sweets does she buy?

2	0
0	0̶
1	1
2̶	2
3	3
4	4
5	5
6	6
7	7
8	8
9	9

Answer: **20**

There are several ways. For example, £20.00 − £2.20 = £17.80; $£0.89 \times 10 = £8.90$; £17.80 − £8.90 = £8.90; so Priya buys 10 + 10 = 20 packs.

Now answer the training question.

Training question

Record your answer on the number grid (right), as shown in the example on the opposite page.

John makes a large cube by gluing together 1 cm cubes.

John's cube has edges of length 6 cm.

How many 1 cm cubes has John used to make his large cube?

The correct answer is at the bottom of this page.

0	0	0
1	1	1
2	2	2
3	3	3
4	4	4
5	5	5
6	6	6
7	7	7
8	8	8
9	9	9

Use the downloaded answer sheet to record your answers to the questions that follow. You will see the examples and training question have already been recorded.

Check your answers only after completing all of Paper 3. The answers are in a cut-out section at the end of the book. Complete the 'results' boxes at the end of this part when you have added up your score. If you run over the time given, complete the questions and note the time you have taken. When you have completed all the questions, record your time in the time box.

You now have 11 minutes to complete the following 16 questions. Start the timer.

1   A rectangle with side lengths of whole centimetres has area 36 cm².
    Which of the following could *not* be the perimeter of the rectangle?   (1)

26 cm	30 cm	40 cm	74 cm	28 cm
A	B	C	D	E

2   Dylan walks $2\frac{1}{2}$ kilometres every day. Which of the following is the best estimate
    of the distance he walks in September?   (1)

60 km	65 km	70 km	75 km	80 km
A	B	C	D	E

3   Simone has five different coloured balls in her pocket. She takes out, at random,
    three of the balls. How many different possible combinations are there?   (1)

6	3	20	60	15
A	B	C	D	E

4   At a rugby match 60% of the people in the crowd are male. There are 20 000 females in
    the crowd. How many people are watching the match?   (1)

50 000	60 000	55 000	65 000	120 000
A	B	C	D	E

5   A piece of stiff wire is bent into the shape of a regular pentagon with sides of 12 cm.
    The wire is straightened out and then bent into the shape of a regular hexagon.
    What is the length of each side of the regular hexagon?   (1)

8 cm	9 cm	10 cm	12 cm	14 cm
A	B	C	D	E

6   In a school the ratio of boys to girls is 7 : 6
    There are 20 more boys than girls.
    How many pupils are at the school?   (1)

200	220	240	260	280
A	B	C	D	E

7   A plan of Fred's garden is drawn to a scale of 1 : 1000
    On the plan, a rectangular lawn measures 2 cm by 2.5 cm.
    What is the area of Fred's lawn in real life?   (1)

50 m²	125 m²	45 m²	450 m²	500 m²
A	B	C	D	E

8   Aisha bakes five dozen muffins to be sold at a fair.
    She sells two-thirds of the muffins at 50p each and then reduces the price by 10%
    for the remaining muffins and sells all of them.
    How much money does she take?   (1)

£29	£28	£26	£32	£30
A	B	C	D	E

9   The total mass of a box of identical bricks is 24.8 kg.
    The mean (average) mass of a brick is 800 grams.
    How many bricks are there in the box?   (1)

10 A clock ticks once every second.

Sally starts counting the ticks at exactly 09:30

She stops counting at exactly 09:45

How many ticks has she counted? (1)

11 Sarah had 45 sweets but has eaten 20% of them.

How many sweets does she have left? (1)

12 What is the smallest 3-digit multiple of 7? (1)

13 Which of the following numbers has the largest number of factors? (1)

           45   46   47   48   49

14 Alice has a 2-litre bottle of lemonade.

She fills eight 180 ml glasses. How many 150 ml glasses could she fill with the remaining lemonade? (1)

15 Five consecutive odd numbers have a sum of 105

What is the smallest of the five numbers? (1)

16 Nicola has twice as many marbles as Mandy and three more than Cleo.

Mandy and Cleo have 18 marbles between them.

How many marbles does Nicola have? (1)

Stop the timer. Record your time in the time box below.

Record your results for Part 5 here.

Score [ ] /16   Time [ ] : [ ]

Record your total score and time for Paper 3 here.

Score [ ] /70   Time [ ] : [ ]

 **Paper 4**

Complete all five parts of this paper to the timings given at the start of each set of questions. Stop the timer after completing each part and start it again after answering the training question in the next part.

Part 1: Number and calculations Section time: 7 minutes

How to answer these questions

All your answers to this part should be recorded on this paper.

Look at the example and then complete the training question. **Do not begin timing yourself until you have finished this page.**

> ### Example question
> Write your answer on the line provided.
> There are 12 inches in a foot.
> How many feet are there in 1008 inches?
> Answer: ___**84 feet**___
> 1008 in ÷ 12 = 84

Now answer the training question.

> ### Training question
> Work out the answer to the question and record your answer, as shown in the example above.
> There are 12 inches in a foot.
> How many feet are there in 780 inches? _____
>
> The correct answer is at the bottom of this page.

Record your answers to the questions that follow on the lines provided.

Check your answers only after completing all of Paper 4. The answers are in a cut-out section at the end of the book. Complete the 'results' boxes at the end of this part when you have added up your score. If you run over the time given, complete the questions and note the time you have taken. When you have completed all the questions, record your time in the time box.

Training question answer: **65 feet**   780 in ÷ 12 = 65

You now have 7 minutes to complete the following 14 questions. Start the timer.

1 Eggs are sold in boxes holding half a dozen eggs. Louise needs 40 eggs so she can bake cakes for a party. Eggs are on special offer.

Eggs
£2.50 per box
Special offer:
3 boxes for the price of 2

  What will Louise pay for the eggs she needs? £_____ (1)

2 Two consecutive prime numbers have a product of 437

  What is the larger number? _____ (1)

3 What is the remainder when 300 is divided by 7? _____ (1)

4 Calculate $(3 \times -2) + 15 - 8$ _____ (1)

5 Write 14.55 correct to one significant figure. _____ (1)

6 Write 54 as a product of its prime factors. _____ (1)

7 Tara is thinking of a 2-digit number less than 40
  The number is one less than a square number and one more than a prime number.

  What number is Tara thinking of? _____ (1)

8 By how much is the square of 8 larger than the square of 7? _____ (1)

9 When Terry tackled a maths test the stopwatch timing him was accurate to the nearest 100th of a second. Terry's time was recorded to the nearest second as 7 minutes 12 seconds.
  What is the maximum time that could have been shown on the watch? _____ (1)

10 What is the sum of the first four multiples of 7? _____ (1)

11 What number is exactly half way between 23 and 141? _____ (1)

12 The number 43 has a digit sum of 7 $(4 + 3 = 7)$
  What is the smallest 7-digit number that has a digit sum of 7? _____ (1)

13 On this part of Paper 4 you are given 7 minutes to answer 14 questions.
  If it takes you an average of 35 seconds to answer a question, how many questions

  will you answer before you are told to stop? _____ (1)

14 What is $14\,000\,000 - 14$? _____ (1)

Stop the timer. Record your time in the time box below.
Now move on to Part 2.
Record your results for Part 1 here *after you have completed the rest of Paper 4.*

Score ___ /14 Time ___ : ___

Part 2: Measures, shape and space

Section time: 11 minutes

How to answer these questions

All your answers to this part should be recorded on this paper.

Look at the example and then complete the training question. **Do not begin timing yourself until you have finished this page.**

Example question

Write your answer on the line provided.

One angle of an isosceles trapezium is 40°

What size is the largest angle?

Answer: **140°**

The angles are 40°, 140°, 140°, 40°

Now answer the training question.

Training question

Work out the answer to the question and record your answer, as shown in the example above.

The interior angle of a regular plane shape is 140°

How many sides does the plane shape have? _____

The correct answer is at the bottom of this page.

Record your answers to the questions that follow on the lines provided.

Check your answers only after completing all of Paper 4. The answers are in a cut-out section at the end of the book. Complete the 'results' boxes at the end of this part when you have added up your score. If you run over the time given, complete the questions and note the time you have taken. When you have completed all the questions, record your time in the time box.

Training question answer: 9 sides   Interior angle 140°; exterior angle 40° (180° − 140°); 360° ÷ 140° = 9

You now have 11 minutes to complete the following 14 questions. Start the timer.

1   How many of the shapes below have rotational symmetry of 2? _____   (1)

2   Two angles of a triangle are 103° and 49°.

    What is the size of the third angle? _____   (1)

3   A circle has circumference 1 m.
    What is the approximate radius of the circle?

    Give your answer in centimetres to the nearest 5 cm. _____   (1)

4   Romilly does a cross-country run of 3.5 km. Her average speed is 15 km/h.
    She starts at 2.00 p.m.

    At what time does she finish? _____   (1)

5   A rectangle is two and a half times as long as it is wide, and the perimeter is 28 cm.

    What is the area of the rectangle? _____   (1)

6   The diagram below shows a regular octagon of side 10 cm.

    24 cm

    What is the area of the regular octagon? _____   (1)

7   The distance between Angleford and Beastly is 24 km (15 miles).
    The distance between Beastly and Crinkly is 165 miles.

    What is this distance in kilometres? _____   (1)

8   Here are three pieces of a puzzle.

    9 cm

    A   B   C

    Piece A has area 81 cm².
    Piece B has area 90 cm².
    What is the area of piece C? _____   (1)

9 What name would be given to a pyramid with a total of six faces? _____ (1)

10 One angle of an isosceles triangle is 102°.

   What size is each of the other two angles? _____ (1)

11 Calculate the area of the parallelogram. _____ (1)

10 cm   14 cm   36 cm

12 The area of the shaded square is 4 cm^2.

not to
scale

   What is the *perimeter* of the large square? _____ (1)

13 Kilt sizes are measured in inches. Hamish's waist measurement is 75 cm.

   Take 30 cm to be the same as 12 inches.

   What size of kilt (in inches) should Hamish order? _____ (1)

14 The pattern of regular hexagons below is drawn on an isometric dotted grid.

   What is the ratio, in its simplest form, of shaded area to

   unshaded area? _____ (1)

**Stop the timer. Record your time in the
time box below.**

Now move on to Part 3.

**Record your results for Part 2 here *after
you have completed the rest of Paper 4.***

Score [   ] /14 Time [   ] : [   ]

Part 3: Applying maths

How to answer these questions

All your answers to this part should be recorded on this paper.

Look at the example and then complete the training question. **Do not begin timing yourself until you have finished this page.**

> ### Example question
> Write your answer on the line provided.
> What is the next number in this sequence?
>
> 1   5   13   29   ...
>
> Answer: __61__
>
> To get from one term to the next, add 4, add 8, add 16, so then add 32 to get 61

Now answer the training question.

> ### Training question
> Work out the answer to the question and record your answer, as shown in the example above.
>
> What is the next number in this sequence?
>
> 1   4   5   9   14   _____
>
> The correct answer is at the bottom of this page.

Record your answers to the questions that follow on the lines provided.

Check your answers only after completing all of Paper 4. The answers are in a cut-out section at the end of the book. Complete the 'results' boxes at the end of this part when you have added up your score. If you run over the time given, complete the questions and note the time you have taken. When you have completed all the questions, record your time in the time box.

You now have 11 minutes to complete the following 16 questions. Start the timer.

1 For a school trip, three buses, each capable of seating 53 passengers, transport the adults and children. There is one adult for every six children.
There are five empty seats.
How many children are on the trip? _____ (1)

2 Lara uses baking trays that will make a dozen buns.

She has an order for 50 buns.
She completely fills enough trays to make at least 50 buns.

Lara supplies the 50 buns ordered. How many buns are left over? _____ (1)

3 A model dinosaur, normally priced at £12.50, is sold at £10.00 in the sale.

What is the percentage reduction in the sale? _____ (1)

4 A family orders three teas, two coffees, a cake and some biscuits.

tea	£1.10
coffee	£1.70
cake	£2.30
biscuit	£0.50

The total bill is exactly £10.00
How many biscuits does the family order? _____ (1)

5 Will, Bea and Violet shared a large bag of chips in the ratio 2:3:5

Bea got 27 chips. How many chips were in the bag? _____ (1)

6 Amanda multiplied her favourite number by 7, then subtracted 4 and finally divided by 3
The result was 8
What is Amanda's favourite number? _____ (1)

7   George has a box containing 24 plastic balls of the same size.
    Five balls are red, six are yellow, four are green and the rest are blue.
    George picks a ball at random from the box.

    Which one of the following is *not* true? _____
    A   He is more likely to pick a yellow ball than a red ball.
    B   He is least likely to pick a green ball.
    C   He is three times as likely to pick a blue ball as a red ball.
    D   He has a one in four chance of picking a yellow ball.
    E   He is most likely to pick a ball that is *not* blue.   (1)

8 Which of the following does *not* give the answer 36? _____

   $108 \div 3$ $1\frac{1}{2} \times 24$ $\frac{3}{5}$ of 65   90% of 40 $10^2 - 8^2$ (1)

9 Ian has a square piece of paper with 80 cm sides.
   He cuts it in half to make two rectangles, and then cuts one rectangle in half to make
   a square.
   He repeats the cutting process to make a smaller rectangle and then a smaller square.

   What is the area of this square? _____   (1)

10 In a card game, a lion scores the same as three hippos and a hippo scores 3 points
   less than a gorilla. A gorilla scores 4 points.
   The four cards in Emma's hand score a total of 12 points.
   Which one of the following groups of four cards does Emma have? _____
   A   lion, lion, hippo, hippo
   B   hippo, hippo, hippo, hippo
   C   lion, hippo, hippo, gorilla
   D   lion, hippo, gorilla, gorilla
   E   lion, lion, lion, gorilla   (1)

11 Gemma's holiday in Spain will cost exactly £970
   Gemma has £789 in the bank and her savings jar contains 93 £1 coins and seven
   £2 coins.
   How much more does Gemma need to save? _____   (1)

12 In the wall of bricks shown below, the number on a brick is the sum of the numbers
   on the two bricks supporting it.

   What number is on the shaded brick? _____   (1)

13 Max plants 270 identical seeds.
   Seven-ninths of the seeds grow into plants.
   How many of the seeds do *not* grow into plants? _____   (1)

14 The diagram shows the floor plan of a room.

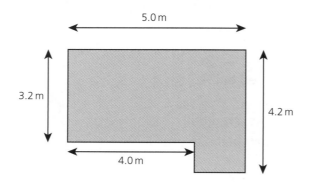

What is the area of the floor? _____ (1)

15 The design below is made up of two regular hexagons and two squares.

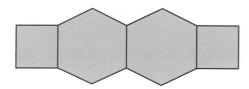

Each square has area 16 cm².
What is the perimeter of the design? _____ (1)

16 Which of the fractions below has the smallest value? _____

$\frac{3}{8}$ $\frac{1}{3}$ $\frac{2}{5}$ $\frac{3}{7}$ $\frac{4}{9}$ $\frac{4}{7}$ (1)

**Stop the timer. Record your time in the time box below.
Now move on to Part 4.
Record your results for Part 3 here *after
you have completed the rest of Paper 4.***

Score [   ] /16   Time [   ]:[   ]

Part 4: Algebra

Record your answers to this part on the lines provided, as shown in the example. Your answers to questions 1 to 8 should be chosen from the table below. No option can be used more than once (so you cannot choose the answer '6' as this is used in the example.

Example question

What is the value of x in the equation $5(x-2)+7=27$?

Answer: ___6___

Check your answers only after completing all of Paper 4. The answers are in a cut-out section at the end of the book. Complete the 'results' boxes at the end of this part when you have added up your score. If you run over the time given, complete the questions and note the time you have taken. When you have completed all the questions, record your time in the time box.

You now have 5 minutes to complete the following 8 questions. Start the timer.

3	A + 3 B × 3	A × 2 B − 3	$3a - 4b$	1
$4a + 6b$	7	6	$-7\frac{1}{2}$	$3a + 4b$
$4a + 11b$	20	10	A × 3 B − 5	−8

1   The function machine has lost its labels for functions A and B. Three input/output pairs are given.

      What are the missing labels? A _____ B _____   (1)

For each of questions 2 to 6, solve the equation to find the unknown number.

2   $3a + 12 = 21$ _____   (1)

3   $3(b - 5) = 45$ _____   (1)

4   $6c + 7 = 4c - 8$ _____   (1)

5   $5(4 - d) = 15$ _____   (1)

6   $e + 2 = \frac{e}{2} - 2$ _____   (1)

For each of questions 7 and 8, simplify the expression as far as possible.

7   $3(2a + 3b) - 2(a - b)$ _____   (1)

8   $a(3 + b) - b(a - 4)$ _____   (1)

Stop the timer. Record your time in the time box below.
Now move on to Part 5.

Record your results for Part 4 here *after* you have completed the rest of Paper 4.

Score [ ] /8   Time [ ] : [ ]

Part 5: Handling data

How to answer these questions

All your answers to this part should be recorded on this paper.

Look at the example and then complete the training question. **Do not begin timing yourself until you have finished this page.**

> ### Example question
> Write your answer on the line provided.
> Clare's scores on five spelling tests were:
>
> 7   8   6   7   7
>
> What was Clare's mean score?
>
> Answer: **7**
>
> The sum of the scores is 35; then 35 ÷ 5 = 7

Now answer the training question.

> ### Training question
> Work out the answer to the question and record your answer, as shown in the example above.
>
> Clare's scores on six mental arithmetic tests were:
>
> 8   9   7   9   10   8
>
> What was her median score? _____
>
> The correct answer is at the bottom of this page.

Record your answers to the questions that follow on the lines provided.

Check your answers only after completing all of Paper 4. The answers are in a cut-out section at the end of the book. Complete the 'results' boxes at the end of this part when you have added up your score. If you run over the time given, complete the questions and note the time you have taken. When you have completed all the questions, record your time in the time box.

Training question answer: 8.5   For an even number of scores, the median is half way between the middle two; the scores in order are 7, 8, 8, 9, 9, 10

64

You now have 11 minutes to complete the following 16 questions. Start the timer.

1 Louise scored the following numbers of runs in her last five cricket matches.

17   0   0   43   0

   What is her median score? _____ (1)

2 About one in every ten people is left-handed.

   When this information is represented as a pie chart, what will be the size of the

   angle representing right-handed people? _____ (1)

3 Olivia, Bell and Clarissa start a game with 18 marbles each.

   In the first round, Olivia wins five marbles from Bell, Bell loses four marbles to Clarissa and Clarissa wins five from Olivia.

   In the second round, Amy loses 11 marbles to Bell, Bell wins nine from Clarissa and Clarissa loses three to Amy.

   How many marbles does Bell have at the end of the game? _____ (1)

Questions 4 to 9 are concerned with the diagram below.
The diagram shows information about the favourite drinks of the members of a sports club.

boys	18	41	16
girls	30	8	32
	Fizz	Sparkle	Bubbles

4 How many members are in the club? _____ (1)

5 How many more boys are there than girls? _____ (1)

6 Which is the most popular drink? _____ (1)

7 What fraction of the children that chose Bubbles are girls? _____ (1)

8 What percentage of the boys chose Fizz? _____ (1)

9 The club decided to buy each member a can of their favourite drink. Sadly, the shop had run out of Bubbles.

   Of the boys who would have had Bubbles, seven chose Fizz and the rest chose Sparkle. All the girls who would have had Bubbles chose Sparkle instead.

   How many cans of Sparkle did the club order altogether? _____ (1)

Questions 10 to 12 are concerned with Liam's numbered discs shown below.

① ② ③ ④ ⑤ ⑥ ⑦ ⑧ ⑨ ⑩

Give your answers as fractions in their lowest terms (simplest form).
10 Liam puts the discs in his pocket and then takes one out at random.

   What is the probability that the disc has a factor of 12 on it? _____ (1)

11 The disc Liam took out was ⑤.

He puts this disc on the table and takes out a second disc from his pocket.

What is the probability that the second disc is *not* a square number or prime

number? _____ (1)

12 The second disc Liam took was ⑧.

He puts this disc on the table and takes out a third disc from his pocket and puts it on the table.

What is the largest possible total of the numbers on the discs left in his pocket?

_____ (1)

Questions 13 to 16 are concerned with the line graph below that shows the journeys of two friends.

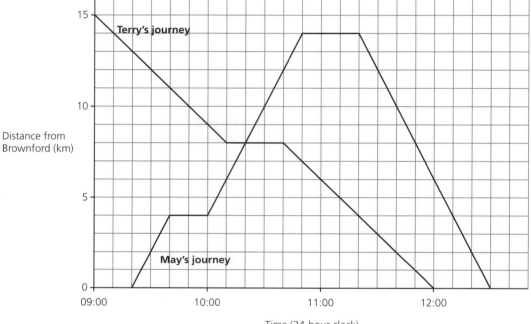

Distance from Brownford (km)

Time (24-hour clock)

13 At what time did May set off from Brownford? _____ (1)

14 How far had Terry travelled before he stopped for a rest? _____ (1)

15 There is a bridge 10 km from Brownford.

How many minutes before May crossed the bridge did Terry cross it? _____ (1)

16 What was May's average speed in km per hour on the return journey to

Brownford? _____ (1)

Stop the timer. Record your time in the time box below.
Record your results for Part 5 here.

Score ☐ /16 Time ☐ : ☐

Record your total score and time for Paper 4 here.

Score ☐ /68 Time ☐ : ☐

Answers

All the references in the boxes below refer to the *11+ Mathematics Revision Guide* (ISBN: 9781471849213) so you know exactly where to find out more about the question and your answer.

11+
Mathematics
Revision Guide
For 11+, pre-test and independent school exams, including CEM, GL and ISEB
Louise Martine
GALORE PARK

PAPER 1

Part 1: Number and calculations

Training question   **D 62**   17 + 107 = 124; 124 ÷ 2 = 62   See pages 12–13 and 24–25.

1   E   **£5.88**   Each chocolate bar costs 2p less than £1; 6 × 2 = 12; 12p less than £6.00

     See pages 24–25 and 50–51.   (1)

2   E   **25**   BIDMAS; 35 − 18 + 8 = 25   See pages 28–29.   (1)

3   C   **88**   Probably easiest to subtract 40 and then add 3   See pages 30–31.   (1)

4   C   **4.96**   4.96 is only 0.04 off 5.00   See pages 14–17.   (1)

5   A   **300**   Look only at the third figure; since this (4) is less than 5, the figure to the left is not increased

     See pages 14–17.   (1)

6   C   **7653**   The 7 represents 7000   See pages 12–13.   (1)

7   D   **3.25**   In order: 3.025, 3.052, 3.25, 3.502, 3.52   See pages 12–13.   (1)

8   D   **1600**   Think of 40 × 40   See pages 14–17.   (1)

9   A   **1541**   Probably best to do: 20 × 67 = 1340; 3 × 67 = 201; 1340 + 201 = 1541   See pages 34–35.   (1)

10   A   **£3.84**   Each pen costs 1p less than 30p; 4 × 30 = 120; 120 − 4 = 116; £1.16 less than £5.00

     See pages 24–25, 32–33 and 50–51.   (1)

11   C   **50 g**   4000 ÷ 80 = 50   See pages 36–37.   (1)

12   B   **2**   The prime numbers are 13 and 41; 9 divides by 3; 49 divides by 7 and 51 divides by 3

     See pages 20–21.   (1)

13   A   **10p**   3 × 24 = 72; £7.20 divided by 72 gives 10p each chocolate   See pages 50–51.   (1)

14   **4**   2 × 12 = 24; 56 − 24 = 32; 32 ÷ 8 = 4   See pages 32–33, 36–37 and 50–51.   (1)

15   **28**   2 + 3 + 5 + 7 + 11 = 28   See pages 18–19.   (1)

16   **24**   24 has eight factors: 1, 2, 3, 4, 6, 8, 12, 24; 28 has six factors and the others each have four factors

     See pages 18–19.   (1)

17   **16**   (0 × 1) + (5 × 1) + (4 × 2) + (1 × 3) = 0 + 5 + 8 + 3 = 16   See pages 24–25.   (1)

18   **36**   17 + 55 = 72; 72 ÷ 2 = 36; check 36 − 17 = 19; 55 − 36 = 19   See pages 12–13.   (1)

19   **13**   40 ÷ 3 = 13 remainder 1   See pages 18–19.   (1)

20   **20**   15 × 7 = 105; 17 × 5 = 85; 105 − 85 = 20   See pages 32–33.   (1)

Part 2: Applying maths

Training question   D **44 cm** $15 + 7 = 22$; $22 \times 2 = 44$ See pages 92–93.

1   B   **2**   Work backwards: $21 \div 3 = 7$; $7 - 5 = 2$ See pages 122–123.   (1)

2   C   **3** $4 + 0 + 4 + 0 + 7 = 15$; $15 \div 5 = 3$ See pages 146–147.   (1)

3   A   **£5.06**   Total cost 6 pence less than £15.00; change 6p more than £5.00   See pages 24–25 and 50–51.   (1)

4   E   **28**   One-quarter of the members are male; $7 \times 4 = 28$ See pages 58–59.   (1)

5   B   **20p and** $3 \times 20p = 60p$; $4 \times 10p = 40p$; $60p + 40p = £1$; 'guess check'; other choices eliminated quickly

       10p   See pages 50–51.   (1)

6   D   **5**   Even numbers divisible by 3; digit sum divisible by 3; 64 and 400 are not divisible by 6

       See pages 36–37.   (1)

7   C   **4**   Make an organised list; 479, 497, 749, 794, 947, 974; four are odd   See pages 12–13.   (1)

8   E   **27** $61 + 88 = 149$; $73 + 49 = 122$; $149 - 122 = 27$ See pages 30–31.   (1)

9   C   **5**   Guess and check: $5 + 7 = 12$; $4 \times 3 = 12$; or algebra: $x + 7 = 3(x - 1)$ leading to $x + 7 = 3x - 3$ then $2x = 10$

       See pages 126–127.   (1)

10   D   **10** $24 \div 7 = 3$ remainder 3, so four trips for sheep; $16 \div 3 = 5$ remainder 1, so six trips for cows; $4 + 6 = 10$ (1)

11   **8** $100 \div 12 = 8$ remainder 4 so she must bake nine times; $9 \times 12 = 108$; $108 - 100 = 8$ (1)

12   **4**   Trial and improvement: $4^2 = 16$; $16 - 4 = 12$ See pages 124–125.   (1)

13   **6**   It is not necessary to complete the whole grid! Top row missing number 9; $17 - 11 = 6$

       See pages 120–121.   (1)

14   **28**   The number of triangles increases by 4 each time: 8, 12, 16, 20, 24, 28   See pages 130–131.   (1)

Part 3: Fractions, proportions and percentages

Training question   C **60%** $\frac{3}{5} = \frac{60}{100}$; multiply numerator and denominator by 20   See pages 54–55.

1   B $\frac{1}{4}$ $\frac{25}{100}$ simplifies; divide both numerator and denominator by 25   See pages 54–55.   (1)

2   A   **372**   Cows 124; sheep 248; total $124 + 248 = 372$ See pages 48–49.   (1)

3   A   **9**   10% of 60 is 6; 5% of 60 is 3; $6 + 3 = 9$ See pages 62–63.   (1)

4   E   **12**   Total shares $1 + 3 = 4$; each share $24 \div 4 = 6$; Angel eats one share, so 6 sweets; Bryony eats

       three shares, so 18 sweets   See pages 46–47.   (1)

5   B   **2:3** $8:12$ simplifies (divide both numbers by 4)   See pages 46–47.   (1)

6   A   **20%**   He has saved one-fifth of the money; $\frac{56}{280} = \frac{2}{10} = \frac{20}{100}$ See pages 64–65.   (1)

7   C $\frac{1}{2}$ Four of the eight equal pieces   See pages 58–59.   (1)

8   B $\frac{1}{4}$ There were 12 slices $(3 + 2 + 1 + 1 + 1 + 4$ left$)$; $\frac{3}{12} = \frac{1}{4}$ See pages 58–59.   (1)

9   B   **30%** $\frac{18}{60} = \frac{3}{10} = \frac{30}{100}$ See pages 54–55.   (1)

10   D   **one-sixth**   Imagine one-third of a pizza cut into two equal slices   See pages 68–69.   (1)

11 C £36 20% is one-fifth; $45 \div 5 = 9$; $45 - 9 = 36$ See pages 64–65. (1)

12 D 10 12 shares (5 + 7); two sweets each share ($24 \div 12$); Tom gets five shares; $5 \times 2 = 10$

See pages 46–67. (1)

13 D 0.8 $\frac{4}{5} = \frac{8}{10}$; multiply numerator and denominator by 2 See pages 52–53. (1)

14 B 120 300×0.4; or $300 \div 100 = 3$, then 3×40 See pages 62–63. (1)

15 B $\frac{1}{2}$ $\frac{4}{9}$ and $\frac{3}{8}$ are both less than one-half; $\frac{2}{3}$ and $\frac{3}{4}$ are both greater than one-half

See pages 42–45 and 56–57. (1)

16 A $5\frac{1}{4}$ $3 \times \frac{3}{4} = \frac{9}{4}$; $\frac{9}{4} = 2\frac{1}{4}$; $2\frac{1}{4} + 3 = 5\frac{1}{4}$ See pages 66–67. (1)

17 C 20 Jack's bucket is one and a half $\left(\frac{3}{2}\right)$ times the capacity of Jill's; Jack will take $\frac{2}{3}$ the number of trips

See pages 62–63. (1)

18 D $\frac{1}{6}$ Two-thirds left; one-quarter of two-thirds is one-sixth See pages 68–69. (1)

Part 4: Handling data

Training question C **240 kg** $5 \times 48 = 240$ See pages 30–31.

1 B **unlikely** Three out of nine; less than even chance See pages 156–157. (1)

2 B **24** Six goats; eight cows; ten sheep; $6 + 8 + 10 = 24$ See pages 138–139. (1)

3 D **8** 13 boys; 19 girls (13 + 6); $19 - 11 = 8$ See pages 134–135. (1)

4 C **£6.00** $2 \times 5 = 10$; $5 \times 10 = 50$; $7 \times 20 = 140$; $2 \times 50 = 100$; $10 + 50 + 140 + 100 = 300$; 300p = £3; £3 + £3 = £6

See pages 140–141. (1)

5 C **One-sixth of the plants are either 3 or 4 cm** All others are false or could be false

See pages 140–141 and 148–149. (1)

6 C **3** Total 21 (1 + 2 + 5 + 4 + 0 + 2 + 7); $21 \div 7 = 3$ See pages 146–147. (1)

7 E **42** In order: 0, 12, 23, [39, 45], 45, 78, 104; the mean of the middle two: $39 + 45 = 84$; $84 \div 2 = 42$

See pages 146–147. (1)

8 D **4** 16 symbols; 12 pupils in class, so four must own both dogs and cats See pages 136–137. (1)

9 C **40** 20% (100 − 30 − 25 − 25); 30% represents 60 trees, so 20% represents 40 trees

See pages 54–55. (1)

10 D **39** $3 \times 0 + 5 \times 1 + 6 \times 2 + 2 \times 3 = 0 + 5 + 12 + 6 = 23$ brothers and sisters; $23 + 16 = 39$ (1)

11 C **The spinner is as likely to land on white as to land on grey.** Grey and white have the same number

of sections See pages 156–157. (1)

12 A **131.8 cm** $143.7 - 11.9 = 131.8$ See pages 146–147. (1)

PAPER 2

Part 1: Applying maths

Training question   **O 19**   The first multiple of 5 is 5 (1×5); $20 \times 5 = 100$; $19 \times 5 = 95$ See pages 18–19.

1   **N**   **10.70**   'Lose' figures to right of second decimal place; look only at third place (the 4); 4 is less than 5 so round down   See pages 14–17.   (1)

2   **L**   **149.31** $0.77 - 0.46 = 0.31$; $166 - 17 = 149$; $149 + 0.31 = 149.31$ See pages 50–51.   (1)

3   **E**   **20%**   £36 − £28.80 = £7.20; $7.20 \times 100 = 720$; $720 \div 36 = 20$ See pages 64–65.   (1)

4   **A**   **11.7** $46.8 \div 4 = 11.7$ See pages 74–75.   (1)

5   **F**   **53**   15:45 to 16:00 is 15 min; $15 + 38 = 53$ See pages 74–75.   (1)

6   **G** $\frac{1}{4}$ $\frac{3}{4}$ left; $\frac{3}{4} \times \frac{1}{3} = \frac{1}{4}$ See pages 58–59.   (1)

7   **S**   **£43.68**   5% of 80p is 4p; next year 84p per week; $52 \times 84p = 4368p$; 4368p is £43.68   See pages 50–51.   (1)

8   **B** $\frac{4}{9}$ $\frac{160}{360}$ simplifies to $\frac{4}{9}$ (divide numerator and denominator by 40)   See pages 42–43 and 50–51.   (1)

9   **R**   **52** $7 \times 7 = 49$; $49 + 3 = 52$ See pages 74–75.   (1)

10   **P**   **112** $11 + 13 + 17 + 19 + 23 + 29 = 112$ See pages 20–21.   (1)

11   **H**   **32** $(4 \times 3) + (2 \times 7) + 6 = 12 + 14 + 6 = 32$ See pages 126–127.   (1)

12   **T**   **36**   The mean (average) is 34 $(102 \div 3)$; numbers are 32, 34 and 36   (1)

13   **L**   **270**   60% are girls; 60% is $\frac{3}{5}$; $450 \div 5 = 90$; $90 \times 3 = 270$ See pages 48–49 and 62–63.   (1)

14   **M**   **57**   £1 is $5 \times 20p$; £11 is $55 \times 20p$; $55 + 2 = 57$ See pages 50–51.   (1)

15   **O**   **4**   Check digit sum divisible by 3; 53 and 1033 are not multiples of 3   See pages 18–19.   (1)

16   **B**   **1** $1 = 1^2$; $1 = 1^3$ See pages 18–19.   (1)

17   **G**   **7**   Work backwards: $26 + 7 = 33$; $33 \div 3 = 11$; $11 - 4 = 7$ See pages 124–125.   (1)

18   **A**   **87**   To get from one term to the next, multiply by 4 and then subtract 5   See pages 124–125.   (1)

Part 2: Measures, shape and space

Training question   **B 5 cm** $30\,cm \times 20\,cm = 600\,cm^2$; $3000\,cm^3 \div 600\,cm^2 = 5\,cm$ See pages 102–103.

1   **B**   **14°** $33 - 19 = 14$; easier to subtract 20 and then add 1   See pages 72–73.   (1)

2   **B**   **132 cm²**   Either $144 - 12$ or $120 + 12$ See pages 94–95.   (1)

3   **B**   **1**   Only the isosceles trapezium (third from left)   See pages 82–83.   (1)

4   **C**   **12 cm** $6 \times 8 = 48$; $48 \div 4 = 12$ See pages 88–89.   (1)

5   **C**   **255 cm**   12 inches in 1 foot; $8 \times 30 = 240$; 6 inches is 15 cm; $240 + 15 = 255$ See pages 72–73.   (1)

6   $\frac{9}{10}$ **litre** $\frac{900}{1000}$ simplifies to $\frac{9}{10}$ (divide numerator and denominator by 100)   See pages 102–103.   (1)

7   **0.2 litre**   Each long division represents 100 ml; two divisions represents 200 ml (0.2 l)   See pages 102–103.   (1)

8   **6 glasses** $\frac{900}{150} = 6$; easy way: $2 \times 150 = 300$; $900 \div 300 = 3$ See pages 102–103.   (1)

9   **isosceles**   Two equal sides; both sides are diagonals of 4×2 rectangles   See pages 80–81.   (1)

| 10 | **6 units²** | Bits of squares combine to form six whole squares | See pages 96–97. | (1) |

11 **translation** Slide each vertex (corner) 3 units to the right and 2 units down See pages 114–115. (1)

12 **(5, 4)** x co-ordinate first See pages 112–113. (1)

Part 3: Number and calculations

Training question **D 12** There are five shares $(2 + 3 = 5)$; there are four sweets in each share $(20 \div 5 = 4)$;

Jill gets three shares, so she gets 12 $(3 \times 4 = 12)$ sweets See pages 36–37 and 46–47.

1 **B 56, 24** $8 \times 7 = 56$; $3 \times 8 = 24$ See pages 32–33. (1)

2 **A 61** To get from one term to the next, multiply by 2 and then add 3 See pages 124–125. (1)

3 **B 140** Must end in 5 or 0, so rule out 57; divide other options by 7 See pages 18–19. (1)

4 **B 10** Eight shares in total $(3 + 5)$; five sweets in each share $(40 \div 8)$; the difference is two shares,

so Lisa gets 10 more See pages 46–49. (1)

5 **C 5** Work backwards: $60 \div 3 = 20$; $20 + 5 = 25$; $25 \div 5 = 5$ See pages 124–125. (1)

6 **D 81** $3 \times 3 \times 3 \times 3$ See pages 19–19. (1)

7 **C 3** 2, 13, and 41 are prime numbers. 9 is 3×3; 49 is 7×7; 51 divides by 3 since digit sum (6)

divides by 3 See pages 20–21. (1)

8 **11** $300 \div 28 = 10$ remainder 20, so 11 cubes needed See pages 36–37. (1)

9 **9** $(5 + 4) \times 3 - 2 = 25$; $5 + (4 \times 3) - 2 = 15$; $5 + 4 \times 3 - 2 = 15$; $5 + 4 \times (3 - 2) = 9$ See pages 28–29. (1)

10 **37** $37 - 17 = 20$; $37 + 17 = 54$; you could use algebra: $a + b = 54$, $a - b = 20$; add the two equations:

$b - b = 0$, $2a = 74$ so $a = 37$ See pages 20–21. (1)

11 **143** $10 \times 13 = 130$; $130 + 13 = 143$ See pages 34–35. (1)

12 **7** £4.48 before change; $448 \div 64 = 7$ (divide by factors, e.g. $\div 4$ then $\div 4$ and finally $\div 4$ again)

 See pages 50–51. (1)

13 **36** $4 \times 9 = 36$; $3 \times 12 = 36$ See pages 36–37. (1)

14 **24** $10 - 2 = 8$; $8 \times 3 = 24$ See pages 122–123. (1)

15 **53.5** Cut off after first decimal place; look only at the figure in the second place (4); if less than

5 round down See pages 14–17. (1)

16 **$7\frac{1}{2}$ (7.5)** One-third of 90 is 30; one-quarter of 30 is 7.5 See pages 68–69. (1)

Part 4: Algebra

Training question **N $7a + 3b$** $3a + 4a = 7a$; $5b - 2b = 3b$ (we 'collect' like terms) See pages 126–127.

1 **D ÷** $39 \div 3 = 13$ See pages 126–127. (1)

2 **L 16** Two identical terms; each half the total; $32 \div 2 = 16$ See pages 128–129. (1)

3 **F $2p + 3$** $p \times 2 = 2p$; $2p + 3$ See pages 122–123. (1)

4 **H $4x + 3y$** Four oranges cost $4x$ pence; three pears cost $3y$ pence See pages 126–127. (1)

5   I   **17−n**   It may help to give a number to *n* and see what happens; suppose *n* is 10, Neil would be 7 (17−10) years old   See pages 128–129.   (1)

6   S   **−1** $(4\times5)-(3\times7)$; 20−21   See pages 126–127.   (1)

7   T   **8**   Using algebra: $p+q=14$; $p-q=2$; add the two equations; $2p=16$, so $p=8$; q is 6 (14−8)   See pages 128–129.   (1)

8   B   **17**   Two numbers with product 60 and difference 7; $60=2\times30$ or 3×20 or 4×15 or 5×12 or 6×10; $5+12=17$ (1)

9   P   **19**   To get from one term to the next, simply add 6   See pages 124–125.   (1)

10   B   **6**   Subtract 3 from both sides   See pages 128–129.   (1)

11   M   **12**   Add 3 to both sides   See pages 128–129.   (1)

12   D   **5**   Subtract 3 from both sides and then divide both sides by 3   See pages 128–129.   (1)

13   J   **9**   Add 3 to both sides and then divide both sides by 2   See pages 128–129.   (1)

14   L   **4**   There are several ways: $4a+6=22$; $4a=16$; $a=4$; or $2a+3=11$; $2a=8$; $a=4$ See pages 128–129.   (1)

15   N   **3**   There are three shaded triangles in every pattern in the sequence   See pages 130–131.   (1)

16   C   **13**   Add 2 when moving from one pattern to the next   See pages 130–131.   (1)

17   H   **33**   Side length 11 units; $3\times11=33$ See pages 130–131.   (1)

18   E   **28**   The numbers go up 1, 6, 15, … ; moving from one term to the next, add 5, then 9, *then 13*, then 17   See pages 130–131.   (1)

PAPER 3

Part 1: Fractions, proportions and percentages

Training question   **48**   10% of 120 is 12, so 40% is 12×4 See pages 62–63.

| 1 | E | **49.8** | In order: 48.9, 49.3, **49.8**, 49.9, 50.1   See pages 56–57. | (1) |

2   E   **0.875**   One-quarter is 0.25; one-eighth is 0.125; seven-eighths is 7×0.125 See pages 52–53.   (1)

3   B   **3**   One-third of $4\frac{1}{2}$ is $1\frac{1}{2}$; $2 \times 1\frac{1}{2} = 3$ See pages 66–67.   (1)

4   C   **60%**   36 girls $(60 - 24)$; $\frac{36}{60} \times 100 = 60$ See pages 62–63.   (1)

5   **14**   70% is equivalent to 7 out of 10   See pages 54–55.   (1)

6   **39**   Look only at the third figure (4 in this case); if this figure is 4 or less, round down *('lose' the figures cut off; 39.00 would be incorrect)*   See pages 14–17.   (1)

7   **72**   60% do not own dogs; 10% of 120 is 12; 60% of 120 is 72 (6×12) See pages 54–55.   (1)

8   **15**   10 shares $(3 + 7)$; five sweets in each share $(50 \div 10)$; Naga gets three shares (3×5) See pages 46–47.   (1)

9   **81** $243 \div 3 = 81$ See pages 58–59.   (1)

10   **770** $220 \div 2 = 110$ grams each person; $110 \times 7 = 770$ See pages 48–49.   (1)

11   **35**   1% of 1000 is 10; $\frac{1}{2}$% of 1000 is 5; $3 \times 10 = 30$; $30 + 5 = 35$ See pages 62–63.   (1)

12   **10**   One-eighth of 400 is 50; one-sixth of 360 is 60; $60 - 50 = 10$ See pages 58–59.   (1)

13   **13**   Add convenient amounts; $3\frac{2}{3} + 5\frac{1}{3} = 9$; $2\frac{1}{4} + 1\frac{3}{4} = 4$; $9 + 4 = 13$; always look for an easier way!   See pages 44–45.   (1)

14   **9**   Possibly 'guess and check' is easiest: 50% would be 7 out of 14   See pages 54–55.   (1)

Part 2: Handling data

Training question   **C 8**   The numbers are 2, 5, 5, 8; the middle two must both be 5 since both the median and the mode are 5; the total must be 20 since the mean is 5 $(4 \times 5 = 20)$; for the range, $8 - 2 = 6$ and no other pair of numbers with a difference of 6 has a sum of 10   See pages 146–147.

1   C   **50** $17 + 7 + 15 + 11 = 50$ See pages 134–135.   (1)

2   A   **32** $17 + 15$ See pages 134–135.   (1)

3   B   **22%**   11 pupils out of the 50; $\frac{11}{50} = \frac{22}{100}$ See pages 54–55 and 134–135.   (1)

4   D   **8**   32 play tennis $(17 + 15)$; 24 play hockey $(17 + 7)$; $32 - 24 = 8$ See pages 134–135.   (1)

5   A   **20** $4 + 6 + 5 + 2 + 3 = 20$ See pages 48–49 and 138–139.   (1)

6   B   **34** $(4 \times 0) + (6 \times 1) + (5 \times 2) + (2 \times 3) + (3 \times 4)$; $0 + 6 + 10 + 6 + 12 = 34$ See pages 138–139.   (1)

7   B   **1**   The most common number of goals scored in a match   See pages 146–147.   (1)

8   B   1.5   10 matches with scores of 0 or 1; 10 matches with scores of 2, 3 or 4; middle two numbers are

1 and 2, so median is 1.5   See pages 146–147.   (1)

9   B $\frac{1}{3}$ Three out of nine   See pages 146–147.   (1)

10   C   2:1   Four grey, two white; 4:2 simplifies to 2:1   See pages 46–47.   (1)

11   E $\frac{5}{9}$ Five of the nine counters are not grey   See pages 156–157.   (1)

12   C $\frac{3}{8}$ Three of the eight remaining counters are black   See pages 156–157.   (1)

13   D   David   Ben 39 kg, David 41 kg   (1)
14   A, B   Alice,   Ben 1.37 m, Flora 1.47 m, Alice 1.48 m,
        Ben   David 1.49 m, Clare 1.54 m, Emily 1.62 m
15   C   Clare   Three have blue eyes: Alice 10:7, Clare 10:9, Emily 10:5; Flora's age is 10:8; Clare is older than Flora   (1)
16   A, E   Alice,   Alice 45 kg, Emily 38 kg;
        Emily   45 + 38 = 83   (1)

Part 3: Number and calculations

Training question   61   One number must be 2 since the total is odd; 63 − 2 = 61; quite often a question is much easier
than it may first appear; a little thinking when you first read a question can save a lot of time

See pages 20–21.

1   C   51   51 has digit sum 6, which is divisible by 3   See pages 20–21.   (1)

2   E   21+16   256 ÷ 8 = 32; 6^2 = 36; 5×7 = 35; $\sqrt{400}$ = 20; 21 + 16 = 37   See pages 18–19 and 36–37.   (1)

3   B   16   80 ÷ 16 = 5; 64 ÷ 16 = 4   See pages 18–19 and 36–37.   (1)

4   D   42   42 ÷ 14 = 3; 42 ÷ 21 = 2   See pages 36–39.   (1)

5   109   11 × 12 = 132; 11 + 12 = 23; 132 − 23 = 109   See pages 34–35.   (1)

6   44   2 for 90p; 4 for £1.80; 40 for £18; 44 for £19.80   See pages 50–51.   (1)

7   2   3×5+4 = 25−8+2 (15 + 4 = 17 + 2)   See pages 18–19, 28–29 and 120–121.   (1)

8   502   502 is 2 off; 497 is 3 off   See pages 14–17.   (1)

9   90   Digit sum must be a multiple of 3   See pages 18–19.   (1)

10   29   The next smallest is 47   See pages 18–19.   (1)

11   27 $27 = 3^3$ See pages 18–19.   (1)

12   250   500 ÷ 250 = 2   See pages 18–19.   (1)

Part 4: Algebra

Training question   C   7a + b   2(a + 2b) = 2a + 4b, then 2a + 5a = 7a and 4b − 3b = b   See pages 126–127.

1   A   5   Work backwards: 58 + 5 = 63; 63 ÷ 7 = 9; 9 − 4 = 5   See pages 124–125.   (1)

2   A   4   Work backwards: 4 + 12 = 16; $\sqrt{16}$ = 4   See pages 18–19 and 124–125.   (1)

3   B   3   Algebra to the rescue! 5c − 12 = c; 4c = 12 (add 12 to both sides and subtract c from both sides); then

divide both sides by 4   See pages 122–127 and 126–127.   (1)

4   E   11   Add the two equations; 2p = 22, so p = 11   See pages 126–129.   (1)

5	C	$\frac{1}{2}$	Divide both sides by 4; 2 divided by 4 is a half See pages 128–129.	(1)
6	A	2	Multiply out brackets first or divide both sides by 3 first See pages 128–129.	(1)
7	D	3	Subtract c from both sides and add 6 to both sides; $4c = 12$, so $c = 3$ See pages 128–129.	(1)
8	E	5	Multiply out brackets first or divide both sides by 2 first; $2d = 10$, so $d = 5$ See pages 128–129.	(1)
9	D	48	One-quarter of e is 12, so $e = 4 \times 12$ See pages 128–129.	(1)
10	D	6	$6f - 18 = 2f + 6$; $4f = 24$; $f = 6$ See pages 128–129.	(1)
11	D	4	$\# = 7 - @$; $2(7 - @) + 3@ = 17$; $14 - 2@ + 3@ = 17$; $@ = 3$ (subtract 14 from both sides), so $\# = 4$ See pages 126–129.	(1)
12	E	6	$6 \times 4 = 24$ and $\frac{6}{4} = 1\frac{1}{2}$ See pages 126–129.	(1)

Part 5: Applying maths

Training question   **216** $6 \times 6 \times 6$ See pages 100–101.

1	E	**28 cm**	6×6 perimeter 24; 4×9 perimeter 26; 3×12 perimeter 30; 2×18 perimeter 40; 1×36 perimeter 74 See pages 86–87 and 92–95.	(1)
2	D	**75 km**	30 days; $30 \times 2 = 60$; $30 \times \frac{1}{2} = 15$; $60 + 15 = 75$ See pages 72–73.	(1)
3	D	**60**	Five ways of choosing the first ball; four ways of choosing the second ball; three ways of choosing the third ball; $5 \times 4 \times 3 = 60$ See pages 156–157.	(1)
4	A	**50 000**	20 000 is 40% of the crowd; $20\,000 \times \frac{100}{40} = 50\,000$ See pages 62–63.	(1)
5	C	**10 cm**	$5 \times 12 = 60$; the wire is 60 cm long; $60 \div 6 = 10$ See pages 88–89.	(1)
6	D	**260**	There are 13 shares; each share is 20 (20 more boys than girls); $13 \times 20 = 260$ See pages 46–47.	(1)
7	E	**500 m²**	Scale 1 cm to 10 m; area 20 m $\times$ 25 m; $20 \times 25 = 500$ See pages 48–49.	(1)
8	A	**£29**	60 muffins (five dozen, 5×12); 40 muffins sold at 50p (£20); 20 sold at 45p (£9); £20 + £9 = £29 See pages 58–59 and 64–65.	(1)
9		**31**	24.8 kg is 24 800 g; $24\,800 \div 800 = 31$ See pages 36–37.	(1)
10		**900**	15 minutes; $15 \times 60 = 900$ See pages 74–75.	(1)
11		**36**	80% are left; 80% is $\frac{4}{5}$; one-fifth of 45 is 9; $4 \times 9 = 36$ See pages 62–63.	(1)
12		**105**	Guess and check: $14 \times 7 = 98$; $15 \times 7 = 105$ See pages 18–19.	(1)
13		**48**	45 has six factors (1, 3, 5, 9, 15, 45); 46 has four (1, 2, 23, 46); 47 has two (1, 47 – prime); 48 has ten (1, 2, 3, 4, 6, 8, 12, 16, 24, 48); 49 has three (1, 7, 49 – square) See pages 18–19.	(1)
14		**3**	$8 \times 180 = 1440$; $2000 - 1440 = 560$; 560 ml left; $3 \times 150 = 450$; $4 \times 150 = 600$, so only three 150 ml glasses See pages 102–103.	(1)
15		**17**	$105 \div 5 = 21$; the middle number is 21, so the numbers are 17, 19, 21, 23, 25	(1)
16		**14**	Algebra to the rescue! $n = 2m$; $n = c + 3$; so $2m = c + 3$; $2m - c = 3$; $m + c = 18$; add last two equations; $3m = 21$, so $m = 7$; we know that $n = 2m$, so $n = 14$; there are several ways of doing this, including 'guess and check' See pages 126–129.	(1)

PAPER 4

Part 1: Number and calculations

Training question **65 feet** $780 \text{ in} \div 12 = 65$ See pages 72–73 and 36–37.

1 **£12.50** Six boxes (36 eggs) cost £10; one box (six eggs) costs £2.50; £10 + £2.50 = £12.50 See pages 50–51. (1)

2 **23** Consecutive primes so each must be about the size of $\sqrt{437}$; $\sqrt{400}$ is 20, so look at the primes either side of 20; 19 and 23 See pages 46–47 and 34–35. (1)

3 **6** $300 \div 7 = 42$ remainder 6 See pages 36–37. (1)

4 **1** $^-6 + 7 = 1$ See pages 26–29. (1)

5 **10** Look only at the second figure (4); this is less than 5 so round down; keep units place by filling with zero See pages 14–17. (1)

6 **2×3^3** $2 \times 3 \times 3 \times 3$ See pages 20–21. (1)

7 **24** Look at numbers one less than a square number (15, 24, 35); check which is one more than a prime number; 24 is one more than the prime number 23 See pages 18–19 and 124–125. (1)

8 **15** $8^2 = 64$; $7^2 = 49$; $64 - 49 = 15$ See pages 18–19. (1)

9 **7 min 12.49 s** It could not be 12.50 seconds because that would be rounded to 13 seconds to the nearest second See pages 74–75. (1)

10 **70** $7 + 14 + 21 + 28 = 70$ See pages 18–19. (1)

11 **82** $23 + 141 = 164$; $164 \div 2 = 82$ See pages 12–13. (1)

12 **1 000 006** The smallest over a million See pages 12–13. (1)

13 **12** 10×35 seconds is 350 seconds (5 min 50 s); 2×35 seconds is 70 seconds (1 min 10 s); $10 + 2 = 12$ questions (5 min 50 s + 1 min 10 s = 7 min) See pages 74–75. (1)

14 **13 999 986** Take care! See pages 30–31. (1)

Part 2: Measures, shape and space

Training question **9 sides** Interior angle 140°; exterior angle 40° (180° − 140°); 360° ÷ 40° = 9 See pages 88–89.

1 **4** The isosceles trapezium (second right) has no rotational symmetry; the 'cross' (far right) has rotational symmetry order 4 See pages 82–83. (1)

2 **28°** 180° − 103° − 49° See pages 108–109. (1)

3 **15 cm** π is a little over 3; diameter approximately 30 cm; so radius is 15 cm See pages 90–91. (1)

4 **2.14 p.m.** 15 km in 60 minutes; 1 km in 4 minutes; 3 km in 12 minutes; 0.5 km in 2 minutes; total time 14 minutes (12 + 2) See pages 76–77. (1)

5 **40 cm²** Perimeter 28 cm; half the perimeter 14 cm; length 10 and width 4 (10 is 2.5 × 4); 10 × 4 = 40 See pages 94–95. (1)

6 **480 cm²** The area of one triangle is $\frac{1}{2} \times 12 \times 10 = 60\,\text{cm}^2$; 8 triangles; $8 \times 60 = 480$ See pages 96–97. (1)

7 **264 km** $165 \div 15 = 11$; distance is 11 times that from Angleford to Beastly; $11 \times 24 = 264$ See pages 72–73. (1)

8 **99 cm²** The pieces are based on a 9×9 square; one extra 'bump' has area $9\,\text{cm}^2$ ($90 - 81$); piece C has two extra 'bumps' ($81 + 18$) See pages 94–95. (1)

9 **pentagonal pyramid** Five sloping, triangular faces; one pentagonal base See pages 100–101. (1)

10 **39°** $180 - 102 = 78$; $78 \div 2 = 39$ (there cannot be another angle of 102!) See pages 108–109. (1)

11 **360 cm²** Base $\times$ perpendicular height; $36 \times 10 = 360$ See pages 96–97. (1)

12 **16 cm** Side of shaded square is 2 cm; side of large square is 4 cm; perimeter of large square is 16 cm See pages 92–95. (1)

13 **30 inches** 30 cm is 12 inches; 60 cm is 24 inches; 15 cm is 6 inches; $24 + 6 = 30$ See pages 72–73. (1)

14 **3 : 1** You can work this out by looking at just one sixth of the large hexagon (there are three little 'triangles' in the shaded area and just one little 'triangle' in the unshaded area) See pages 48–49. (1)

Part 3: Applying maths

Training question 23 Add the previous two terms to get the next; $9 + 14 = 23$ See pages 124–125.

1 **132** 159 seats; groups of 7 (1 adult + 6 children); 154 occupied seats ($159 - 5$); $154 \div 7 = 22$; $6 \times 22 = 132$ See pages 48–49. (1)

2 **10** 12 buns at a time; five bakings needed ($4 \times 12 = 48 \rightarrow 2$ buns short); $60 - 50 = 10$ (1)

3 **20%** Price reduced by £2.50; one-fifth off; $\frac{250}{1250} \times 100 = 20$ See pages 64–65. (1)

4 **2** Three teas £3.30; two coffees £3.40; one cake £2.30; total of these £9.00; £10.00 − £9.00 = £1.00; two biscuits £1.00 See pages 50–51. (1)

5 **90** Total shares 10 ($2 + 3 + 5$); three shares is 27 chips ($\times 9$) so 10 shares is 90 See pages 46–47. (1)

6 **4** Work backwards: $8 \times 3 = 24$; $24 + 4 = 28$; $28 \div 7 = 4$ See pages 124–125. (1)

7 **C** There are 9 blue balls; probability of picking a yellow ball is $\frac{1}{24}$ which simplifies to $\frac{1}{4}$ See pages 156–157. (1)

8 **$\frac{3}{5}$ of 65** $108 \div 3 = 36$; $1\frac{1}{2} \times 24 = 36$; $\frac{3}{5}$ of $65 = 39$; 90% of $40 = 36$; $10^2 - 8^2 = 36$ ($100 - 64$)

See pages 18–19, 36–37, 58–59, 62–63 and 66–67. (1)

9 **400 cm²** Rectangle 80×40; square 40×40; rectangle 40×20; square 20×20; area $400\,\text{cm}^2$ See pages 94–95. (1)

10 **D** A scores 8 points; B scores 4 points; C scores 9 points; D scores 12 points; E scores 13 points (1)

11 **£74** $789 + 93 + 14 = 896$; $970 - 896 = 74$ See pages 50–51. (1)

12 **9** Algebra to the rescue! Call the number on the shaded brick x; next row is $3 + x$, $2 + x$, 6; next row is $5 + 2x$, $8 + x$; $13 + 3x = 40$; $3x = 27$; $x = 9$ See pages 120–121. (1)

13 **60** Two-ninths do *not* grow; $\frac{2}{9} \times 270 = 60$ See pages 58–59. (1)

14	**17 m²**	$5 \times 4.2 = 21$; $4 \times 1 = 4$; $21 - 4 = 17$ See pages 94–95.	(1)
15	**56 cm**	You really need do only half and then $\times 2$! See pages 94–95.	(1)
16	$\frac{1}{3}$	All of the others are close to $\frac{1}{2}$ See pages 42–43.	(1)

Part 4: Algebra

1	**A×3, B−5**	'Guess and check' is possibly the most effective See pages 122–123.	(1)
2	**3**	Subtract 12 from both sides; then divide by 3; $3a = 9$; $a = 3$ See pages 128–129.	(1)
3	**20**	$3b - 15 = 45$; $3b = 60$; $b = 20$ or $b - 5 = 15$ so $b = 20$ See pages 128–129.	(1)
4	$-7\frac{1}{2}$	$2c = {}^-15$ See pages 128–129.	(1)
5	**1**	$4 - d = 3$; $1 = d$ See pages 128–129.	(1)
6	$^-8$	$2e + 4 = e - 2$; $e = {}^-8$ See pages 128–129.	(1)
7	**$4a + 11b$**	$6a + 9b - 2a + 2b = 4a + 11b$ See pages 126–127.	(1)
8	**$3a + 4b$**	$3a + ab - ab + 4b = 3a + 4b$ (remember ab is the same as ba) See pages 126–127.	(1)

Part 5: Handling data

Training question	**8.5**	For an even number of scores, the median is half way between the middle two; the scores in order are 7, 8, **8, 9**, 9, 10 See pages 146–147.	
1	**0**	In order: 0, 0, **0**, 17, 43; median is middle value See pages 146–147.	(1)
2	**324°**	$360 \div 10 = 36$; left-handed 36; right-handed 324 (9×36) See pages 142–143.	(1)
3	**29**	You need look at Bell only! $18 - 5 - 4 + 11 + 9$	(1)
4	**145**	Add all the numbers	(1)
5	**5**	75 boys; 70 girls; $75 - 70 = 5$	(1)
6	**Sparkle**	49 compared to 48 for each of the other two drinks See pages 146–147.	(1)
7	$\frac{2}{3}$	32 of the 48 See pages 58–59.	(1)
8	**24%**	$\frac{78}{75} \times 100$ See pages 62–63.	(1)
9	**90**	9 (boys) + 32 (girls) = 41 extra; $49 + 41 = 90$	(1)
10	$\frac{1}{2}$	Factors of 12 are 1, 2, 3, 4, 6 (five out of ten) See pages 18–19 and 156–157.	(1)
11	$\frac{1}{3}$	Discs 6, 8 and 10 only (three out of nine) See pages 18–19 and 156–157.	(1)
12	**41**	5 and 8 are not there; if he picks 1, then the discs left are 2, 3, 4, 6, 7, 9, 10; $2 + 3 + 4 + 6 + 7 + 9 + 10 = 41$	(1)
13	**09:20**	10 minutes each division See pages 74–75 and 150–151.	(1)
14	**7 km**	From 15 km to 8 km from Brownford See pages 150–151.	(1)
15	**40 min**	Terry crossed the bridge at 09:50; May crossed the bridge at 10:30 See pages 74–75 and 150–151.	(1)
16	**12 km/h**	Look at how far she travelled in one hour, e.g. from 11:30 to 12:30 See pages 76–77.	(1)